Exploring Okinawa
The History, Culture and Lifestyle of Japan's Southern Islands

Yuki Kobayashi

English translated by Kamil Spychalski

Special Edition

JN094939

IBC パブリッシング

はじめに

　ラダーシリーズは、「はしご（ladder）」を使って一歩一歩上を目指すように、学習者の実力に合わせ、無理なくステップアップできるよう開発された英文リーダーのシリーズです。

　リーディング力をつけるためには、繰り返したくさん読むこと、いわゆる「多読」がもっとも効果的な学習法であると言われています。多読では、「1. 速く　2. 訳さず英語のまま　3. なるべく辞書を使わず」に読むことが大切です。スピードを計るなど、速く読むよう心がけましょう（たとえば TOEIC® テストの音声スピードはおよそ 1 分間に 150語です）。そして 1 語ずつ訳すのではなく、英語を英語のまま理解するくせをつけるようにします。こうして読み続けるうちに語感がついてきて、だんだんと英語が理解できるようになるのです。まずは、ラダーシリーズの中からあなたのレベルに合った本を選び、少しずつ英文に慣れ親しんでください。たくさんの本を手にとるうちに、英文書がすらすら読めるようになってくるはずです。

《本シリーズの特徴》

- 中学校レベルから中級者レベルまで5段階に分かれています。自分に合ったレベルからスタートしてください。
- クラシックから現代文学、ノンフィクション、ビジネスと幅広いジャンルを扱っています。あなたの興味に合わせてタイトルを選べます。
- 巻末のワードリストで、いつでもどこでも単語の意味を確認できます。レベル1、2では、文中の全ての単語が、レベル3以上は中学校レベル外の単語が掲載されています。
- カバーにヘッドホーンマークのついているタイトルは、オーディオ・サポートがあります。ウェブから購入／ダウンロードし、リスニング教材としても併用できます。

《使用語彙について》

レベル1：中学校で学習する単語約1000語

レベル2：レベル1の単語＋使用頻度の高い単語約300語

レベル3：レベル1の単語＋使用頻度の高い単語約600語

レベル4：レベル1の単語＋使用頻度の高い単語約1000語

レベル5：語彙制限なし

スペシャル・エディション：レベル3〜4に相応。ただし、中学英語レベルでも無理なく読めるよう巻末のワードリストには全単語の意味を掲載しています。

Table of Contents

Exploring Okinawa

The History, Culture and Lifestyle of Japan's Southern Islands

読み始める前に

青く透き通った海に浮かぶ沖縄県。琉球王国の宮廷文化、貿易を行ったアジア各地の文化、日本本土の文化など、その歴史と共に多様な文化が織りなす独自性を築き上げてきました。沖縄がこれまで歩んできた歴史、今の姿や暮らし、そしてこれからについて、そのすべてを英語で読み進めていきましょう。

沖縄県の県章

沖縄県基本情報

県庁所在地：那覇市

面積：2,281.12km²（47都道府県中44番目）

人口：約144万人（47都道府県中25番目・2017年）

沖縄県の花：デイゴ　*Tiger's claw*

沖縄県の木：リュウキュウマツ　*Ryukyu Island pine*

沖縄県の鳥：ノグチゲラ　*Okinawa woodpecker*

沖縄県の魚：タカサゴ（グルクン）　*Double-lined fusilier*

気候と地形：沖縄県は日本の南西、九州と台湾の間に位置し、広い海に散在する島嶼群から成り立っています。2018年現在、160ある島のうち沖縄本島、宮古島、石垣島、西表島など47の島に人が住んでいます。

気候は一年を通して温暖（年平均気温23.1℃）で、最高気温が30℃を超える真夏日が100日以上になる年もあります。他県と比べて降水量が多いのも特徴です。台風の通り道にあたることから、6〜10月の間、年平均で7〜8回も台風が接近します。これに備えて、周りを木や石垣で囲い、屋根を平らにしたコンクリートの家が多いのです。

友好提携都市：国外では、アメリカ・ハワイ州、ブラジル・南マットグロッソ州、ボリビア・サンタクルス州、中国・福建省と姉妹提携宣言をしています。また国内では、兵庫県および福島県と提携して、相互交流事業を行っています。

Preface

From the edge of Alaska to tropical New Guinea, the western half of the Pacific Ocean is decorated by a necklace of islands. Among the accents on this necklace are Japan, Taiwan, the Philippines, and Indonesia, but there are also countless small diamonds. Okinawa, once called Ryukyu, is among the most beautiful of these small islands.

Long ago, people navigated throughout the islands of the Western Pacific. Northern tribes journeyed from Siberia, and other groups sailed from southern Asia. Just as the Greeks traveled throughout the Aegean Sea, so these sailors voyaged around the Pacific, moving from island to island. Eventually, the various peoples settled all of the islands, mingling with other groups and creating their own kingdoms. Ryukyu was no exception and was once an independent realm called the Ryukyu Kingdom.

From the beginning of the Ryukyu Kingdom in the fifteenth century, envoys were sent to China. The people also created a unique island culture that was influenced by both Japan and China. The people spoke a language that is considered to be one of the roots of the Japanese language. Unfortunately, this language is now endangered, but for linguists and archaeologists, it is a treasure trove of information about ancient oceanic civilizations. Scholars are now turning to Okinawa to gather evidence regarding how the technology of rice production expanded in the Far East, and to learn how southern Asian culture influenced Japan, Korea, and beyond.

From ancient times until the medieval era, Ryukyu thrived as a trading center connecting north, east, south, and west due to its strategic location in the southern part of the East China Sea.

Many Chinese, Southeast Asians, Japanese, and later Western sailors identified the Ryukyu Kingdom as the intersection of east Asia, sailing up to Japan along with the warm current. And in winter, when the Siberian anticyclone caused winds to blow southward, people raised their sails and traveled from Japan to regions in southern Asia.

However, in the seventeenth century, Japan expanded and the Ryukyu Kingdom was conquered by the lord of Satsuma, one of the most influential men in the Japanese Shogunate. Okinawa was eventually annexed by Japan in 1879.

Since then, however, Okinawa has maintained its unique island culture even though it is part of Japan. Even to this day, there are various folkcrafts, folk songs, dances, and foods that cannot be found on the mainland.

In the twentieth century, Okinawa was tossed upon the waves of fate due to international power struggles. In the Pacific War, Okinawa was attacked by the American military. It was the only part of Japan that experienced real fighting between Japanese and Americans.

And after the war was over, Okinawa fell under US control for many years. Even now, there are many US military bases in Okinawa. It is an ironic fate for Okinawa due to its strategic location close to China and Southeast Asia.

Okinawa is an incredible blend of island culture and spectacular nature that must be preserved. Now, however, the coral and mangrove of southern islands are in danger due to climate change. The unique culture and ecosystems of these islands are not only part of Japan's heritage, but also the heritage of humanity.

Chapter 1
An Overview of Okinawa

Cape Manzamo (top),
Nakagusuku Castle built by the Ryukyu Kingdom (bottom)

【沖縄県の概要】

　沖縄県は日本全国で4番目に小さく、大小160の島々から成り立っています。地域は大きく、「沖縄本島周辺」、宮古島がある「宮古圏域」、石垣島や西表島がある「八重山地域」の3つに分かれます。透き通った青い海に囲まれた景観はもちろん、沖縄本島の中でも、那覇の中心地は都会的、琉球王国時代の面影を残す首里、自然豊かな北部地域など、さまざまな雰囲気が楽しめる県です。

●わからない語は巻末のワードリストで確認しましょう。

☐ region	☐ tip
☐ birth rate	☐ subtropical
☐ coral	☐ typhoon

●主な地名および名称、固有名詞

☐ Okinawa Island	沖縄本島
☐ Miyako Island	宮古島
☐ Yaeyama region	八重山地域
☐ Ishigaki Island	石垣島
☐ Iriomote Island	西表島
☐ Iheya Island	伊平屋島
☐ Hateruma Island	波照間島
☐ Kitadaito Island	北大東島
☐ Yonaguni Island	与那国島

Miyako Island, located
300 kilometers south of
Okinawa Main Island

Located in the southwest of Japan, Okinawa is the country's fourth-smallest prefecture with an area of around 2,281km^2, just 0.6 percent of the country. The prefecture is made up of 160 islands of various sizes, with people living on just 47 (as of January 2018). These are divided into three main regions—the Okinawa Islands; the Miyako region, which includes Miyako Island; and the Yaeyama region, including the islands of Ishigaki and Iriomote. Okinawa Prefecture covers a vast stretch of ocean, with some 1,000 km from Iheya Island in the north to Hateruma Island in the south, and around 400 km between the islands of Kitadaito in the east and Yonaguni in the west. Hateruma and Yonaguni are also the southern and western tips of Japan.

As of 2018, Okinawa Prefecture had a population of around 1.48 million. While the total population of Japan is falling as people get older and have fewer children, the population of Okinawa is rising every year. This is thanks to a higher birth rate than other prefectures, along with the many people coming to live in Okinawa. In fact, the population of Okinawa is growing faster than anywhere else in Japan except Tokyo (2018).

Okinawa's climate is subtropical, with an average temperature of over 20°C. Being warm year-round makes the oceans around Okinawa a perfect place for corals to grow.

Okinawa's official flower, Deigo

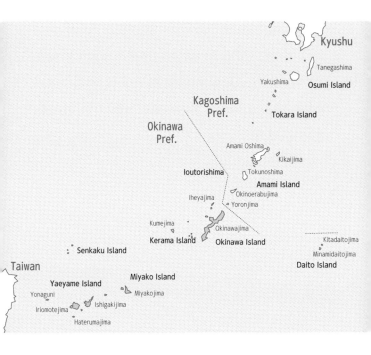

Another feature of Okinawa's climate is the many typhoons. Between June and October, typhoons form in tropical seas and slowly travel north. These typhoons often pass through Okinawa, which lies along their path, at times causing great damage. This is why

Okinawans have always planted trees and built stone walls to protect their homes from typhoon winds. These days, many houses are made of reinforced concrete, which is strong against typhoons.

Iriomote Island, Okinawa's second largest island

Chapter 2
History of Okinawa

Nakamura house built in around mid 18th century (top),
Himeyuri Memorial Tower (bottom)

【沖縄の歴史】

　1429年、尚巴志が覇権を争っていた各地の有力者を統一して琉球王国が成立し、アジア各地との中継貿易によって栄えました。1609年に薩摩藩からの侵攻を受けると、約250年にわたり支配が続きます。明治維新後の1879年、「琉球処分」により沖縄県に改められました。第二次世界大戦終結から27年の間アメリカ領となり、1972年に日本に復帰しましたが、現在も県内各地に米軍基地が存続しています。

●わからない語は巻末のワードリストで確認しましょう。

- □ continent
- □ castle
- □ mainland
- □ shell
- □ UNESCO World Heritage Site
- □ military base

●主な地名および名称、固有名詞

□ Nansei Islands	南西諸島
□ Nakadomari ruins	仲泊遺跡
□ Onna Village	恩納村
□ Uken shell mounds	宇堅貝塚
□ Uruma City	うるま市
□ Nakabaru ruins	仲原遺跡
□ Ikei Island	伊計島
□ Gusuku period	グスク時代
□ Ryukyu Kingdom	琉球王国
□ Sanzan period	三山時代
□ Sho Hashi	尚巴志
□ Shuri Castle	首里城
□ Kanamaru	金丸
□ Satsuma Domain	薩摩藩
□ Sho Taikyu	尚泰久
□ Sho Toku	尚徳
□ Sho En	尚円
□ Amami	奄美
□ Naha	那覇

Ancient Okinawa

People began living on the islands of Okinawa some 20,000–30,000 years ago. At that time, the level of the world's oceans was lower than it is now, so the islands were connected to China by land. It is thought that people came to Okinawa from the continent. Back then, people lived in caves or simple huts and hunted large animals, such as mammoths or moose. This is known as the Prehistoric period.

The Prehistoric period was followed by Okinawa shell heap culture, from around 5,000 B.C. until the 12th century. Shells became so important during this period that it is also known as the Age of Shells. Shells were used as money in China, and cowrie shells from Okinawa's Miyako Island have been found among important Chinese ruins. Many accessories made with shells from Okinawa's oceans have also been found in Kyushu and Honshu. This suggests that valuable shells were used to trade with places such as China, the Nansei Islands, and even Kyushu.

Early in this period, the people of Okinawa were fishermen living along the coast. From there, they gradually moved into the hills and caves, where they made pit homes and began living in groups. By the second half of the period, people were forming large communities in higher inland areas. We believe these lifestyle changes came about because the higher ground was better for farming than the sandy areas near the coast. Clay pottery, stone axes and coffins from the shell heap culture period

Ancient rock dwelling site
(Nakadomari)

have been found at the Nakadomari ruins
(now Onna Village) and Uken shell mounds
(now Uruma City) on Okinawa Island, as well
as the Nakabaru ruins on Ikei Island.

Gusuku Period—Beginnings of the Ryukyu Kingdom

The shift from hunting, fishing and gathering
plants to a lifestyle based on farming (12th–
15th centuries) is known as the Gusuku
period. Gusuku is an Okinawan word that
means "castle." Around this time, people
began living on the higher ground formed by

Ryukyu limestone (rocks created by a build-up of corals and shells), where they farmed crops such as rice, wheat and millet. It is likely that they also began raising cows at the same

One of the Gusuku Sites, Nakijin Castle

time. This stable way of life allowed people to start trading with nearby areas, enabling their political and cultural reach to grow. Around the 14th century, the region's *aji* rulers built forts to expand their power. Large gusuku were built in the three kingdoms on Okinawa Island during what is known as the Sanzan (Three-Kingdoms) period (1322–1429).

The three kingdoms continued to fight for power until Sho Hashi (1372–1439) was able to unite them in 1429. This was the beginning of the Ryukyu Kingdom, which ruled Okinawa for the next 450 years until 1879. Shuri Castle, one of Okinawa's famous tourist spots, was the home of the Sho family. In 2000, the castle became a UNESCO World Heritage Site due to its unique mix of Chinese and Japanese building styles. Its bright red walls represented the Ryukyu Kingdom. Sadly, much of the castle was destroyed by a fire on 31 October 2019. Although it will take time, the prefecture plans to rebuild Shuri Castle so that it can continue to be a symbol of Okinawa into the future.

Shuri Castle registered as part of the UNESCO World Heritage Site Gusuku Sites and Related Properties of Ryukyu Kingdom

Rise and Fall of the Ryukyu Kingdom

Even after Sho Hashi's death, the Sho family continued to rule the kingdom, helping it grow through trade with China, Japan, Korea, and other countries in Southeast Asia. The kingdom imported Chinese spices, silk threads and fabrics to sell to Japan, while goods such as swords, lacquer, and fans were traded in the other direction. Conveniently located between these two countries, the kingdom grew rich as goods were traded through the area.

This prosperity lasted a long time, until two momentous events changed the Ryukyu Kingdom's fate. The first was when Kanamaru (1415–1476) grabbed control of the kingdom, and the second was an invasion of Ryukyu by the Satsuma Domain.

King Sho En
(1415–1475)

Born into a family of farmers on Izena Island, Kanamaru was an intelligent man. His talents led him to serve Sho Taikyu (1415–60), who became the sixth ruler of the Ryukyu Kingdom. After Taikyu's death, Kanamaru held important posts during the rule of the next king, Sho Toku (1441–69), but trouble between them forced him to leave. Sho Toku ruled single-handedly, ignoring the opinions of others and punishing people who had done nothing wrong. Although Sho Toku died young, those who served him had learned their lesson—the next king would not be someone from the Sho family. Kanamaru was called back to Shuri Castle and, partly by force, took over as king. He chose to carry on the Sho family name, calling himself Sho En. The period from Sho Hashi to Sho Toku is known as the First Sho Dynasty (1406–69); Sho En began the Second Sho Dynasty (1469–1879), which lasted until the fall of the Ryukyu Kingdom under the 19th king, Sho Tai.

King Sho Tai (1843–1901)

In the second major change, Okinawa came under the control of the Shimazu clan of Satsuma Domain. Around the 16th century, a rivalry arose between the Ryukyu Kingdom and the Satsuma Domain, which is now Kagoshima Prefecture. In 1606 the Edo shogunate, Japan's central government, allowed the Satsuma Domain to send troops to the Amami Islands and Ryukyu. Three years later, one hundred ships sailed from Satsuma to attack the kingdom. Before long, they took Shuri Castle in Naha and the king, Sho Nei (1564–1620), was forced to surrender.

With the Ryukyu Kingdom under their control, the Shimazu clan began by checking the land to work out how much rice, fabric and brown sugar the people must pay each

King Sho Nei
(1564–1620)

year. The clan also created 15 rules that the Ryukyu Kingdom had to obey. These rules banned trade with other countries and any business activities not approved by the Shimazu clan.

The Satsuma Domain ruled over the Ryukyu Kingdom for around 250 years until the end of the Edo period. The Ryukyu government was allowed to remain, although without any real power. This was done to keep the kingdom's relationship with China, which did not know about Satsuma's control over the islands. In this way, the kingdom continued trading with China, while the Edo shogunate and the Satsuma Domain enjoyed the profits.

The Ryukyuan embassy of 1710

From Ryukyu Kingdom to Okinawa Prefecture

With the fall of the shogunate and the end of the Edo period (1603–1867), Japan entered the Meiji period (1868–1912). In 1871, the Meiji government replaced the old domains with prefectures, and tried to break up the Ryukyu Kingdom at the same time. Naturally, the kingdom wished to continue as its own country, but the Meiji government, partly by force, turned it into Okinawa Prefecture. The official change took place in April 1879.

The Ryukyu government did not simply let this happen, secretly looking to China for help. For their part, Chinese rulers could not accept Japan making Okinawa a prefecture. The two countries began talks around July 1879, but could not agree. Eventually, Japan's victory in the First Sino–Japanese War (1894–95) put an end to the issue.

So how did the local people live after Okinawa became a prefecture?

The prefecture's government created many policies aimed at making Okinawa like the rest of Japan, spreading culture from the mainland to replace traditional Ryukyu culture, including language and customs. For example, the government saw education was a key first step. They set up more than ten elementary schools, as well as interpreter schools where students learned standard Japanese (spoken on the mainland) to become interpreters or teachers.

Then in 1898, a law forcing Okinawans into the army came into effect. Those with high positions in Okinawa Prefecture welcomed this as a way to become close with the

Japanese, but of course ordinary people did not want to go to war. Some faked disabilities or even injured themselves to avoid going into the army. Around this time, the number of Okinawans moving abroad to places like Hawaii or the Philippines also began to increase. Some were people trying to avoid army service, while others moved to find new jobs.

From 1914, Japan entered a brief period of prosperity during the First World War. This included Okinawa, where the sugar industry gained greatly from the world's high sugar prices. However, the good times did not last long—starting in 1929, the Great Depression brought great economic hardship. With few resources, Okinawa struggled to provide food and pay national taxes as people steadily became poorer. As food ran out, some were forced to eat wild palms that contained poison. This miserable situation became known as *sotetsu-jigoku* (palm hell).

Okinawa and World War II

In the 1930s, Japan's relationship with China grew worse, leading to the Manchurian Incident and the Second Sino–Japanese War. As a result, education in Japan began to focus more on loyalty to the nation and the military. This included Okinawa, where ordinary junior and senior high schools held military training almost daily. Japan was on the path to becoming a military power.

As this was happening, World War II began, with Japan being involved from 1941 to 1945. In Okinawa, the war's impact was felt more strongly from around 1944. In

March that year, a force was set up to protect the islands, and many troops were sent to Okinawa. In July, the government created a plan to get Okinawan people off the islands, and the following month three ships left Naha. By then, however, American troops were already nearby. One of the ships, *Tsushima Maru*, sank after being attacked by an American submarine. Some 1,500 lives were lost, including those of schoolchildren.

This was followed by the bombing of 10 October, in which 90 percent of Naha was destroyed, and the landing of American troops on the Kerama Islands. Okinawa found itself in a weak position. On 1 April 1945, American soldiers finally came to Okinawa Island, leading to fierce ground fighting. The sight of flying bullets was described as a "typhoon of steel," which tells the intensity

Marines of the US landing
a beachhead, March 31, 1945

of the battles that took place. The people of
Okinawa were left with few options, and
many even chose to take their own lives.

On 23 June 1945, Japan's top officers killed
themselves, and the long war finally came to
an end on 15 August. In Okinawa, 23 June is
now Memorial Day, when services are held
throughout the prefecture to remember those
who died in the war and to pray for peace.

Okinawa under US Control

After World War II, Okinawa came under

American control and, for a period of 27 years until 1972, was not part of Japan. While the rest of Japan recovered after the war, not much was done to rebuild Okinawa. A proper policy for governing Okinawa was only put in place some five years after the war's end. In 1950, control of Okinawa passed from the military government to the United States Civil Administration of the Ryukyu Islands (USCAR). America began building full-scale military bases, as well as public projects to provide electricity, water, and banking. Profits from these projects were used to help build more facilities.

In 1952, the rest of Japan became free again through the Treaty of San Francisco, but Okinawa stayed under American control. That same year, a new Government of the Ryukyu Islands was given power over the three branches of government, but with all of its members supervised by USCAR.

With the Treaty of San Francisco ending America's hold over Japan, all land used by the US military was to be returned under international law. However, America used its powers to forcefully take land so that it could keep its bases in Okinawa. People who did not agree to lend their land had it flattened by bulldozers. The land was taken on unfair terms, with owners receiving very little in rent.

With their lives affected by American rule, Okinawans also struggled economically during this period. It is even said that people who had lost everything took metal from destroyed planes to make pots, kettles or washtubs.

Later, Okinawa was used as a point for

sending soldiers to war in Korea and Vietnam. This strengthened Okinawan feelings against America, and the movement to return Okinawa to Japan grew. Okinawans worked for a complete and immediate return, wanting peaceful islands with no army bases. However, an agreement between Japan and America in November 1969 let the US keep its bases when Okinawa was handed back three years later in 1972. And so, Okinawa became part of Japan again on 15 May 1972, but the wishes of its people were not fulfilled.

Okinawa since the End of US Control

After rejoining Japan, Okinawa worked to close the gap with the mainland by improving areas such as farms, roads and monorails. Okinawa also changed its currency from the

US dollar to yen. In 1978, the traffic rules were also changed so that cars would drive on the left side instead of the right, with many road signs being replaced. The return to Japan also changed the lifestyles of Okinawans in many ways. As the economy grew, living standards improved greatly since the 1970s and 1980s, almost erasing the gap between Okinawa and mainland Japan. Yet even now, the incomes are still only around 70 percent of the Japanese average, the lowest in the country. The reasons for this include a lack of manufacturing and a large number of people working in services such as tourism and restaurants.

Okinawa and Military Bases

It is fair to say that military bases are at the

Marine Corps Air Station Futenma located in Ginowan

core of Okinawa's history since the end of the war. Under the US-Japan Security Treaty of 1951, America kept its bases even after returning Okinawa to Japan. Even now, US troops remain in Okinawa, which is home to more than 70 percent of the American military facilities in Japan. The fact that Okinawa Prefecture makes up only 0.6 percent of Japan's land area and 1 percent of its population gives a good idea of just how large this number is. While bases create jobs, they also cause problems such as noise, plane crashes, and crime by American soldiers. Even though Okinawans have long fought for fewer bases, unfortunately the burden remains much the same. Solving the problem of Okinawa's bases requires close talks between the governments of Japan, America, and the prefecture.

Okinawa's beautiful sea

Chapter 3
Okinawan Culture

Ruins of Nakijin Castle (top),
Ruins of Katsuren Castle (bottom)

【沖縄の文化】

　かつて琉球王国として中国や朝鮮、東南アジア等との交流が活発だった沖縄は、伝統的な芸能や工芸、行事に至るまで、諸外国の影響を受けながら、独特の文化を育んできました。また、古くから伝わる信仰や思想をもとに、祖先や親族、地域の人々との繋がりを大切にする県民性も受け継がれています。沖縄を訪れる際は、目や耳で、そして心で、こうした文化の一つひとつを感じてみたいものです。

●わからない語は巻末のワードリストで確認しましょう。

☐ worship　　　　　　　☐ cooking fire
☐ ancestor　　　　　　　☐ grave
☐ folk song　　　　　　 ☐ pottery

●主な地名および名称、固有名詞

☐ utaki	御嶽
☐ Hinukan	ヒヌカン
☐ Nirai Kanai	ニライカナイ
☐ Nuchidu Takara	命どぅ宝
☐ Juuruku Nichi	ジュウルクニチ
☐ Shiimii	シーミー
☐ Yukka Nu Hii	ユッカヌヒー
☐ Haarii	ハーリー
☐ Itoman	糸満
☐ Kachashi	カチャーシー
☐ yachimun	やちむん
☐ Tsuboya	壺屋
☐ Yomitan	読谷
☐ Kumejima	久米島
☐ minsa	ミンサー
☐ uchinanchu	うちなーんちゅ
☐ Kumiodori	組踊
☐ Paantu	パーントゥ

38

Utaki Culture and Okinawan Religion

Since ancient times, Okinawans have believed in the gods of *utaki*. To islanders, utaki are holy places found in nearly every Okinawan village. Aside from the main island, utaki culture also exists in places such as the Miyako and Yaeyama Islands. Although utaki take the place of shrines and temples found in other parts of Japan, most are no more than small shrines or carved stones. Unlike Shinto

Okinawa's sacred place, *Utaki*

shrines, there are no large buildings, boxes for offering money, or stone lion statues.

Utaki have been worshipped by local people over many generations, with each area having its own rules. For example, many utaki are in forests, and people are banned from cutting down plants that grow nearby. This creates thick forests around the utaki, hiding them from people passing by on the roads. Other utaki do not allow women or people from outside the village to enter. Since most of these rules are not written down, visiting tourists must take care.

The fire god Hinukan is also worshipped in Okinawan homes. Items such as incense, flowers, small tables, teacups, and sake cups are usually placed near the cooking fire in the kitchen as offerings to Hinukan. The women of each family offer prayers to Hinukan, who guards the home. Hinukan can also communicate with other gods and ancestors, which is why people offer their prayers through Hinukan when they are unable to visit family graves.

Nirai Kanai and Nuchidu Takara

The concepts of Nirai Kanai and Nuchidu Takara are very important to the people of Okinawa.

In Okinawa and the Amami region, Nirai Kanai is believed to be a paradise that lies beyond the ocean or at the bottom of the sea. Legends say that every year, gods from this place visit the world of humans to bring good harvests and prosperity. Nirai Kanai is also mentioned in old writings from the Ryukyu Kingdom. Some areas hold ceremonies to greet the gods on the beaches, or events in which people dressed as gods appear. For this reason, Okinawans are said to show kindness to those who come across the ocean, welcoming people who are not from the islands.

Nuchidu Takara means "life is a treasure," and being alive is what is important. After the horrors of World War II, the people of Okinawa have come to value life and peace so that the same mistakes are not repeated. Even now, children at Okinawan schools often perform a play about the war called "Nuchidu Takara—Ring the Bells of Peace."

Okinawa Prefectural Peace Memorial Museum

Okinawa's Traditional Events

Alongside the normal calendar, Japan's old (lunar) calendar is also used in Okinawa. This old calendar is based on the cycles of the moon. With dates from both calendars being celebrated, many events are held throughout the year in Okinawa. The timing of these events also differs slightly from the rest of Japan. For example, while New Year's Day falls on January 1 in the new calendar, Okinawa also celebrates the lunar New Year about a month later. By the old calendar, January 16 is an event called "Ancestors at the New Year" (known locally as Juuruku Nichi), when people take food to their family graves. The large number of events related to ancestors is a unique part of Okinawa. Based on the old calendar, in early March people gather to share meals in front of family graves during the Shiimii festival, while July 13–15 is the Okinawan version of Obon.

The Shiimii festival is said to have come from China. Families gather in different places, with some coming together in front of gravestones while others hold feasts by small shrines in the mountains. On the day before Shiimii, the mothers in each family can be seen working hard to prepare food for the festival. Layered food boxes are packed with colorful traditional Okinawan dishes including pork, rice cakes and *kamaboko*. These foods are offered and eaten together with ancestors, making the event an important way to bring families closer together.

Another famous event is Yukka Nu Hii, held on May 4 by the old calendar, which is also Children's Day in Okinawa. This event, which also came from China, involves races in boats called Haarii (or Haaree). These

Traditional boat racing, Naha Haarii

races are held in every region to pray for a good catch and safety at sea, but the most famous are the Naha Haarii and the Itoman Haaree. Many locals and tourists come to watch. Larger boats called Haryu Sen are used in the Naha Haarii, while the Itoman Haaree uses traditional *sabani* fishing boats. These small differences between regions are another interesting part of the event.

Ryukyu Folk Songs & Dances

Okinawa is one of Japan's most lively areas of song and dance. Reasons for this include not only Okinawan folk songs, but also the popularity of court music and dance culture during the Ryukyu period. Over time, this passed down to ordinary people, combining with older folk songs to form Okinawa's music culture.

A key part of Okinawan music is the *sanshin*, an instrument with three strings and snakeskin stretched across its body. It was first played in the Ryukyu court, but over time spread among ordinary people. For most, hearing the sanshin's unique sound brings to mind Okinawa. One feature of the sanshin is that its music does not use the regular scale. Known as the *kunkunshi*, "Ai, Otsu, Ro, Shi, Jo, Chu, Shaku, Ko" are used in place of "Do-Re-Mi."

Okinawa's Ryukyu dance is divided into classic, common, and creative dances. Classic dance is the traditional style that was performed in the court of the Ryukyu Kingdom. Later, when Okinawa became a prefecture, classic dance was mixed with the culture of ordinary people to create a new style—common dance. Creative dance is the name for styles created after the war.

Another dance unique to Okinawa is Kachashi, which is a feature of many occasions, such as festivals, celebrations and parties. Kachashi is an Okinawan word that means "to mix." Through song and dance, emotions are mixed and shared with everyone else. Dancers raise both hands—fists for men

Okinawa's traditional dance, Ryukyuan Dance, was designated as a National Important Intangible Cultural Property

and open palms for women—and sway them with the rhythm.

There is also the Eisa, danced in Okinawa during Obon to the rhythm of a small drum called a *paarankuu*. The style of this dance varies by region. Groups of young people start practicing up to a month before the night of Obon, when they dance through local streets. The flexible and dynamic rhythm of lines of Eisa dancers moving as one is a magnificent sight.

Eisa folk dance

Traditional Crafts of Okinawa

Okinawan pottery, known as *yachimun*, has

a history of around 500 years. It is thought that production methods were passed down when ceramics were brought from China and Southeast Asia as part of trade during the Ryukyu Kingdom period. Yachimun pottery has unique coloring and texture, giving it a character not seen outside of Okinawa. On the main Okinawan island, the areas of Tsuboya and Yomitan are well known for yachimun. Yachimun items include plates, sake and tea sets, as well as the traditional *shisa* lion statues found throughout Okinawa.

Around the same time as yachimun, the craft of dyeing fabrics was also brought to the islands from abroad. Protected by the Ryukyu government, the craft grew and changed in ways unique to Okinawa. There are various types, with each area using their own methods.

Types of traditional dyed fabrics in Okinawa

- Ryukyu *bingata*
- Ryukyu *kasuri*
- Kumejima *tsumugi* silk
- Banana fiber cloth
- Miyako ramie
- *Minsa*
- *Hanaori*

Traditional *bingata* fabric

Okinawa textile, *Minsa*, was believed to protect the person who received it

Created around the 15th century, Ryukyu *bingata* is Okinawa's only traditional dyeing method still practiced today. It uses pigments, plant dyes, and Ryukyu indigo, creating brilliantly bright colors. *Minsa* fabric is made using cotton thread, with the Yomitanza and Yaeyama minsa being the most well-known. Although minsa once meant weaving thin sashes for kimono, these days the same methods are used to make items such as bags and wallets.

Although not as old as Okinawa's pottery and dyed fabrics, Ryukyu glass is another popular souvenir. Beginning in the Meiji period, this glass was made into medicine bottles and lamp chimneys (glass tubes to shield flames). Later, cola and beer bottles used by the US military were recycled to make colored glass. While this glass would normally not be used because of air bubbles or thickness, such things were seen as unique, and the items became popular souvenirs among American military personnel. This is still true today, as Ryukyu glass has grown into one of Okinawa's most well-known souvenirs.

Uchinanchu around the World

Uchinanchu means "people of Okinawa," including island residents and those who have moved outside the prefecture. There are said to be more than 400,000 uchinanchu living outside of Okinawa. As we have seen, Okinawans began moving overseas around 1890, at first mostly to Hawaii and mainland America. Later, after Japan's relationship with the US grew worse, more people moved to Brazil, Peru and other parts of South America.

Every five years, Okinawa Prefecture invites Okinawans and their families living abroad to attend a Worldwide Uchinanchu Festival. The first festival was held in 1990, with 2,397 people coming from 17 countries. This big event strengthens the bonds between Okinawans and offers people from many countries a chance to mix. With the sixth festival held in 2016, the total number of Uchinanchu who have visited from around the world reached 26,000. At that event, October 30 was named World Uchinanchu Day to further strengthen the connections between Okinawan people living in the prefecture and around the globe.

Okinawans also moved to other parts of Japan. For example, part of the Tsurumi area in Kanagawa Prefecture is called "Little Okinawa" because of the many Okinawans living there. Many people moved to Tsurumi for work around the time that Japan's economy was growing quickly, when Okinawa Prefecture remained less well-off. While work conditions were certainly not great, with language problems and Okinawans being treated differently, people from the prefecture survived by creating a community and helping each other. Tsurumi is now home to their children and grandchildren, with some Uchinanchu even returning to the area after moving to South America. Their shared history strengthens the bonds between Okinawan people, with the spirit of helping each other still alive today.

Okinawa's World Heritage Sites

The "Gusuku Sites and Related Properties of

the Kingdom of Ryukyu" in Okinawa have been registered as UNESCO World Heritage Sites. These nine sites are made up of five gusuku (castle ruins) and four ruins from the Ryukyu Kingdom.

Okinawa's World Heritage Sites

- Shuri Castle ruins
- Nakijin Castle ruins
- Zakimi Castle ruins
- Katsuren Castle ruins
- Nakagusuku Castle ruins
- Sefa Utaki
- Shikina-en
- Sonohyan Utaki stone gate
- Tamaudun

Zakimi Castle

Chinese-style bridge in Shikina-en

Shuri Castle was the base of the Ryukyu government. It was destroyed during the war in 1945, then rebuilt in 1992. In October 2019, the castle's main buildings were again destroyed by fire; many people hope to see it rebuilt once more. While the other gusuku sites do not have castle buildings, parts such as stone walls and gates remain. All these remains are global treasures, made with unique Ryukyu building styles and methods. The Sefa Utaki, another registered site, is one of the Ryukyu Kingdom's most important sacred places. In the past, only women were allowed to enter. It is also thought to have been the site of ceremonies to appoint the Kingdom's highest priestesses. Items found at Sefa Utaki, including beads, coins and pottery, have been named Important Cultural Properties of Japan. Other sites that form the

World Heritage registration are also related to the Ryukyu Kingdom, including Shikina-en, the site of a royal home, and Tamaudun, built as a royal tomb during the Second Sho Dynasty.

Aside from these sites, Okinawa also has two forms of UNESCO Intangible Cultural Heritage. One is Kumiodori, registered in 2010. Combining dialogue with traditional Okinawan music and dance, Kumiodori was used to entertain official visitors from China. The other is Raiho-shin, registered in 2018. During this traditional community event, people in masks and costumes visit local houses, scolding the lazy and praying for the happiness of those who live there. In 2018, ten Raiho-shin festivals from around Japan were chosen for World Heritage registration, with Okinawa's Paantu among them. Paantu are strange-looking gods, covered in mud and wearing masks, who go around villages to bring luck and chase away evil.

Paantu at Miyakojima City Museum

Chapter 4
The Okinawan Lifestyle

Okinawa's typical Tapas-style restaurant (top),
Okinawa specialty, *goya* (bottom left) and Adan fruit
(bottom right)

【沖縄の暮らし】

　沖縄では、普段の食事で病気の治療や予防をする「医食同源」という考え方から、太陽の光を浴びた野菜や果物、美しい海の幸を用いた栄養バランスのよい料理が作られます。また、タイ米と黒麹菌から作られる蒸留酒「泡盛」も特産の一つです。観光関連産業の成長著しい沖縄ですが、今後はこうした食文化の輸出拡大や沖縄ブランドの確立による、さらなる成長が期待されます。

●わからない語は巻末のワードリストで確認しましょう。

□ nutritional	□ harden
□ aging	□ brewery
□ cave	□ dialect

●主な地名および名称、固有名詞

□ rafute	ラフテー
□ tebichi	テビチ
□ mimiga	ミミガー
□ goya	ゴーヤー
□ nigari	ニガリ
□ mibai	ミーバイ
□ irabucha	イラブチャー
□ gurukun	グルクン
□ awamori	泡盛
□ kusu	古酒（クース）
□ Commodore Perry	ペリー提督
□ otori	オトーリ
□ Cape Maeda	真栄田岬
□ kucha	クチャ
□ Ishiganto	石敢當
□ majimun	マジムン
□ Taketomi Island	竹富島
□ Irabu (Island)	伊良部島
□ Kurima (Island)	来間島
□ Ikema (Island)	池間島

Okinawan Food

Since ancient times, Okinawan meals have been made with a good balance of food grown on farms and found in the wild. With an excellent nutritional balance, Okinawan food culture is full of wisdom for surviving the hot climate.

Okinawans eat a lot of pork, which is used in dishes such as *rafute* (stewed pork rib), *tebichi* (pork leg) and *mimiga* (pig's ear). There is even an old saying that the only part of the pig that can't be eaten is its oink.

Okinawa also has unique fruits and vegetables. Traditional vegetables known as *shima yasai* (island vegetables) include *goya* (bitter melon), *nigana* (bitter greens) and *fuchiba* (mugwort), all of which are very healthy with high nutritional value. Many of the fruits grown in Okinawa have the bright coloring often seen in tropical areas, including dragon fruit, mangos, bananas and papayas. Okinawa's rich sunshine gives these fruits very sweet flavors.

Okinawans also eat a lot of tofu. While tofu has recently become popular around the world, Okinawan tofu, known as *shima dofu* (island tofu), is drier and firmer than that eaten in the rest of Japan. A key part of making regular tofu is nigari, a rich salt that makes the soybean proteins harden, but for shima dofu this is replaced with seawater. The nigari in seawater gives the tofu its shape, along with a nice salty flavor. While shima dofu is made to harden, when left soft and fluffy it is known as *yushi dofu*. This is also often found on Okinawan dining tables, with a gentle flavor that mixes a slight saltiness with the sweetness of soybeans.

At the same time, Okinawa's oceans are also a rich source of food. The islands' warm waters are home to many colorful fish, such as the *mibai*, *irabucha*, and *gurukun*, Okinawa's prefectural fish. The oceans provide not only fish but also many types of seaweed. These include *umi budo* (sea grapes), *asa* (sea lettuce), and *mozuku*, all of which are thought to promote health for longer life.

Okinawa and Alcohol

Okinawa's best-known alcoholic drink is *awamori*. It is made from Thai rice, which is fermented by adding black *koji* mold, before being distilled. There is also special awamori called *kusu*. To be marked as kusu, a product must be mostly awamori that has been aged for at least three years. Leaving awamori to age improves the flavor and gives it a smoother feel. This practice of aging is one of the things that gives awamori its charm.

Awamori was first made around the 15th century. During the Ryukyu Kingdom period, production came under government control. In the Edo period, awamori was sent to the shogunate as part of the Ryukyu Kingdom's payments. Even Commodore Perry, who urged Japan to open its doors to the world, is said to have tried awamori when visiting the Ryukyus. The written report of his journey describes Perry drinking awamori, which he found to be full and thick, like French liqueur.

Later, as the Ryukyu Kingdom became Okinawa Prefecture during the Meiji period, awamori production slowly moved to private businesses. There now 47 breweries in the prefecture, both on the main island and remote islands such as Miyako, Ishigaki, and Kume, continuing to make awamori using traditional methods.

Miyako Island has a unique way of drinking awamori, called *otori*. People sit in a circle with one of the party guests as the parent (*oya*), who makes a speech and drinks their cup of awamori in one go. They refill the cup and pass it to the next person, who drinks the alcohol without speaking. The drinker passes the cup back to the parent, who repeats the same thing with everyone in the circle. After a full round, the cup is passed to the next parent. Alcohol is passed around again and again until everyone in the circle has been the parent. The final speech is very important, with silence required until the finish.

However, since a peak of around 28 million liters in 2004, the amount of awamori sold has been falling each year. National and local governments are working to stop this trend with efforts such as boosting the awamori brand and lowering alcohol taxes. While it is normally taken straight or with ice, a growing number of cocktails are helping a wider range of drinkers to enjoy awamori.

Okinawan Sports

Starting from Tokyo 2020, karate will be part of the Olympic Games. The sport places great importance on etiquette, beginning and ending with bows. But did you know that karate actually began in Okinawa? It is said to come from self-defense learned by samurai families during the Ryukyu Kingdom period. Later trade with China brought this form of self-defense together with Chinese martial arts to create Okinawan karate. With its roots in self-defense, Okinawan karate was not based on the idea of matches, but rather personal growth. However, as it slowly spread throughout Japan, karate developed into the sport it is today, now practiced in more than 150 countries.

Baseball is also popular in Okinawa. The prefecture hosts winter camps for professional teams, and baseball culture has deep roots among its people. Okinawa is also strong in high school baseball, with Konan High School winning both the spring and summer competitions in 2010. With other professional teams including the Ryukyu Golden Kings (basketball) and FC Ryukyu (soccer), Okinawans can be considered as sport-loving people.

Okinawa's Economy & Business

A feature of Okinawa's economy is a large services sector, which makes up more than 80 percent of the prefecture's businesses. This includes areas such as trade and finance, as well as the rapidly growing tourism industry. In 2018, the number of tourists visiting Okinawa rose to around 10 million, more than double the number 15 years ago. Among them are many foreign visitors from Asia, Europe and America. This is partly due to more international cruise ships and low-cost airlines coming to the islands.

More than anything else, people visit Okinawa for its white-sand beaches and beautiful blue ocean. Visitors can enjoy a wide range of water sports, from diving and snorkeling to parasailing. In winter there are also whale-watching tours. One particularly popular diving spot is the Blue Cave in Cape Maeda on Okinawa's main island. Sunlight shining through the cave's entrance reflects to give the entire space a beautiful blue glow. Another spot off Yonaguni Island, known as the Yonaguni Monument, looks like an ancient underwater city. There are doorways, terraces, and steps, but whether these are really ancient ruins or natural formations remains unknown.

New luxury hotels continue to open on Okinawa's main island, as well as islands such as Miyako and Ishigaki that can be reached by direct flights from Tokyo. At the same time, Okinawa's warm climate and low cost of living mean that a large number of travelers choose longer stays in local guest houses. One reason that so many visitors have been drawn to Okinawa is this choice of travel styles.

Even as Okinawa bustles with tourists all year round, life for local people is far from easy. In Okinawa, income per person is around 2 million yen per year. This is low compared to an average of some 3 million yen for Japan as a whole. Reasons for this include an economy that relies on public works and low added value. After being returned to Japan, Okinawa received aid from both national and local governments. As a result, private business grew slowly, and for a long time the economy needed government support. This is seen in the fact that Okinawan companies are less profitable than the Japanese average.

In recent years, Okinawa has been working

towards an economy that can support itself. The prefectural government has laid out a plan that looks beyond Japan to other countries in Asia, with a focus on growth in five areas—international shipping, tourist resorts, air travel, information technology, and new manufacturing.

Although it is a small part of Okinawa's economy, the resources sector is also working to boost exports and add more value to products from farming, forestry, and fishing. With the popularity of Japanese food overseas, the key will be to make Okinawan brands more well-known. Okinawa's closeness to countries in Southeast Asia makes it easier to export very fresh vegetables and seafood. By using its position as the most southern part of Japan, Okinawa hopes for greater growth in the future.

Okinawan Buildings

The main feature of Okinawan houses is that they are built with typhoons in mind. Concrete is used to make buildings strong, and stone fences are built around homes. Inside the fences, people plant trees to shield their homes from strong winds. Roofs are often laid with red tiles, which are made using a clay called *kucha* that is only found in Okinawa. Kucha is formed from the remains of shells and corals piling up over a long time. Although kucha is gray, minerals in the soil change to the red tile

Dating from the 18th century, Nakamura house is a traditional Okinawa style house

color when heated. Red roof tiles are excellent at letting air pass through and giving off heat, which makes them ideal for the harsh heat of Okinawa. Tiles are also joined together with plaster to stop them from coming loose during typhoons.

Walking along the streets of Okinawa, one can often find stones or plaques with three Chinese characters, which are read *Ishiganto*. Ishiganto are placed on fences or walls to protect homes from evil spirits called *majimun*. In many cases, they are placed where three roads meet or streets end

Ishiganto, the ornamental stone tablet seen in Okinawa

in a T. This is because majimun have trouble turning corners, so they run straight into the ishiganto and are destroyed. The ishiganto custom could once be found all over Japan, but now remain mostly in Okinawa and Kagoshima prefectures.

Another well-known Okinawan object is the *shisa* or lion-like statues placed on the roofs and gates of homes. This is also done to keep away evil spirits. They are often displayed as a pair, the male with an open mouth and the female with mouth closed.

The guardian lions of Okinawa, *Shisa*

They watch over the area, bringing good luck and stopping bad things from entering.

Okinawan Dialects

An interesting thing about Okinawa is that, even in the same prefecture, the culture changes slightly from island to island. One example is language. While most Okinawans can now speak standard Japanese, in the past the language differed in each area or island. For example, "thank you" is "nife debiru" on the main island, but "tandiga tandi" on Miyako Island, "nifaiyu" on Ishigaki, and "fugarasa" on Yonaguni Island. It is easy to see that the languages are completely different.

With the increasing use of standard Japanese, fewer people are speaking local dialects. It is even predicted that some languages will disappear in the future. Five of Okinawa's dialects are listed in the "Atlas of the World's Languages in Danger," published by UNESCO. Of these, the languages of Yaeyama and Yonaguni are "severely endangered," while the Miyako, Kunigami and Okinawa languages are "definitely endangered." An area's language represents the lifestyle of its people; efforts to protect and save these languages are important for passing on the cultures of these islands.

Okinawa's Remote Islands

As mentioned before, Okinawa is made up of 160 islands of various sizes. In this section we will look at some of the prefecture's remote islands.

The first is Ishigaki Island. Located in the Yaeyama Islands, Ishigaki is the prefecture's third-largest island. At its center is Okinawa's highest peak, Mount Omoto (526 m). The island's mountains and ocean create a rich natural environment. Ishigaki can be reached by plane from Okinawa's main island in about one hour.

A ten-minute ferry ride from Ishigaki is Taketomi Island. The area's traditional red-tiled homes have been marked for protection as some of Japan's important historic buildings. Taketomi has a population of around 300. With a coastline less than 10 km long, it is possible to walk around the whole island. The views of hibiscus flowers beside white sand paths won't be found anywhere else.

Between Okinawa's main island and Ishigaki are the Miyako Islands. This is a group of eight manned islands, including Miyako, Irabu, and Kurima. The water around the Miyako Islands is some of the clearest in Okinawa, known for its beauty as "Miyako blue." Miyako Island is connected by bridges to three nearby islands—Ikema (bridge opened in 1992), Kurima (opened in 1995), and Irabu (completed in 2015). The Irabu Ohashi connecting Miyako and Irabu is the longest toll-free bridge in Japan. In 2019, an airport will also open on Shimoji Island, which is linked to Irabu. As access has improved in the past few years, the number of Japanese and foreign visitors to the Miyako Islands has greatly increased.

Chapter 5
Natural Environment

Gajumaru trees (top),
Pineapple Field (bottom)

【沖縄の自然】

　沖縄は自然豊かな島です。「美ら海」と呼ばれる世界で随一の透明度を誇る海域には、数多くのサンゴ礁群があります。沖縄本島北部に広がる「やんばるの森」や西表島には希少な自然環境が残存し、独自の生態系が築かれてきました。しかし近年では、地球温暖化による気候変動や、大規模な開発による森林減少と赤土の海域流出が表面化し、沖縄の貴重な自然資源が脅かされています。

●わからない語は巻末のワードリストで確認しましょう。

　　□ abundant　　　　　　　□ plenty of
　　□ ecosystem　　　　　　 □ creature
　　□ global warming　　　　□ red soil

●主な地名および名称、固有名詞

　　□ churaumi　　　　　　　　美ら海
　　□ Yanbaru forest　　　　　やんばるの森
　　□ Okinawa rail　　　　　　 ヤンバルクイナ
　　□ Okinawa woodpecker　 ノグチゲラ
　　□ Ryukyu spiny rat　　　　アマミトゲネズミ
　　□ Urauchi River　　　　　　浦内川

The Iriomote cat
living exclusively
on Iriomote Island

Okinawa's Abundant Nature

The islands of Okinawa have a rich environment, with plenty of ocean, mountains and rivers, as well as untouched natural resources. Okinawa has some of the world's clearest waters, known locally as *churaumi* (clear beautiful ocean). Many coral reefs exist in the area, which is said to be home to more than 200 types of coral.

On land, diverse ecosystems can be found around mountains and rivers. One example is the Yanbaru forest that stretches across the northern part of Okinawa's main island. This special place is home to many natural monuments of Japan, including the Okinawa rail, the Okinawa woodpecker, and the Ryukyu spiny rat. Many creatures that live there cannot be found anywhere else. One of the reasons for the Yanbaru forest's environment is that it was mostly able to escape damage during the war. Thanks to Okinawa's sub-tropical climate, the area also receives a large amount of rain year-round. Few places at the same latitude (27 degrees north) have similar conditions. Over many years, a unique eco-system was created in this rare environment.

Another place known for its precious natural environment is Iriomote Island, some 400 km south-west from Okinawa's main island. The entire island of Iriomote is a national park. Like the Yanbaru forest, this area gets a lot of rain. The Urauchi River that flows through Iriomote is the longest in Okinawa Prefecture and holds vast volumes of water. Mangrove forests stretch across the river's lower reaches, with canoe tours popular among tourists visiting the island.

Environmental Issues in Okinawa

While Okinawa's oceans are known for having many types of coral, bleaching has become a recent problem. There are thought to be various causes, one of which is global warming. In the past 100 years, the waters around Japan have grown about 1.1 degrees warmer, which has changed the currents and begun to affect the weather. Because corals are very weak against environmental change, the possibility that warming has changed their growth conditions cannot be denied.

One cause thought to be even greater than warming is red soil. Found in Okinawa and the Amami Islands, this reddish-brown soil has very small grains. Okinawa receives a lot of rain; each time, the top layers of soil are washed into rivers, which carry the soil to the ocean. In the past, forests stopped red soil from being washed away, but the problem has grown worse as large public works and resort developments reduce the area of forests. The red soil does not actually contain anything that causes harm, but the fine grains take a long time to sink to the bottom, muddying the ocean. This stops the corals from getting the sunlight they need, causing them to die from lack of nutrients. Although rules were set up in 1994 to stop red soil, the problem is still not completely solved.

Hatenohama Beach
with 360 degree ocean view

Word List

A

□ **a** 冠 ①1つの，1人の，ある ②～につき

□ **able** 形 《be – to ～》(人が)～することができる ②能力のある

□ **about** 副 ①およそ，約 ②まわりに，あたりを **come about** 起こる 前 ①～について ②～のまわりに[の]

□ **abroad** 副 海外で[に] **from abroad** 海外から

□ **abundant** 形 豊富な，たくさんの

□ **accept** 動 ①受け入れる ②同意する，認める

□ **accent** 名 アクセント，特徴

□ **access** 名 交通の便，アクセス

□ **accessory** 名 付属品，装飾品，アクセサリー

□ **across** 前 ～を渡って，～の向こう側に，(身体の一部に)かけて **come across** ～を渡って来る 副 渡って，向こう側に

□ **activity** 名 活動，活気

□ **actually** 副 実際に，本当に，実は

□ **adan** 名 アダン《トゲのある葉が特徴の小高木で，夏になると甘い香りを放つ橙色の果実をつける》

□ **add** 動 加える，足す

□ **administration** 名 管理，統治，政権

□ **Aegean Sea** エーゲ海

□ **affect** 動 影響する

□ **after** 前 ①～の後に[で]，～の次に ②《前後に名詞がきて》次々に～，何度も～《反復・継続を表す》 副 後に[で] 接 (～した)後に[で] 動 ～の後を追って，～を捜して

□ **again** 副 再び，もう一度 **again and again** 何度も繰り返して

□ **against** 前 ～に対して，～に反対して

□ **age** 名 時代，年代 動 ～を熟成させる，～を寝かす

□ **Age of Shells** 《the –》貝の時代

□ **aging** 名 熟成

□ **ago** 副 ～前に

□ **agree** 動 ①同意する ②意見が一致する

□ **agreement** 名 ①合意，協定 ②一致

□ **Ai, Otsu, Ro, Shi, Jo, Chu, Shaku, Ko** 工工四(三線の記譜法)の音階

□ **aid** 名 援助(者)，助け

- [ ] **aim** 動ねらう, 目指す
- [ ] **air** 名①《the –》空中, 空間 ②空気,《the –》大気 ③雰囲気, 様子 **air station** 航空基地
- [ ] **airline** 名航空会社
- [ ] **airport** 名空港
- [ ] **aji** 名按司《琉球諸島に存在した称号および位階の一つ》
- [ ] **Alaska** 名アラスカ(州)
- [ ] **alcohol** 名アルコール
- [ ] **alcoholic** 形アルコールの, アルコール性の
- [ ] **alive** 形①生きている ②活気のある, 生き生きとした
- [ ] **all** 形すべての, ～中 **all over** ～中で, ～の至る所で **all year** 一年中, 一年を通して 代全部, すべて(のもの[人]) 名全体 副まったく, すっかり
- [ ] **allow** 動①許す,《– … to ～》…が～するのを可能にする, …に～させておく ②与える
- [ ] **almost** 副ほとんど, もう少しで(～するところ)
- [ ] **along** 前～に沿って 副～に沿って, 前へ, 進んで **along with** ～と一緒に **walk along** ～に沿って歩く
- [ ] **alongside** 前～のそばに, ～と並んで
- [ ] **already** 副すでに, もう
- [ ] **also** 副～も(また), ～も同様に 接その上, さらに
- [ ] **although** 接～だけれども, ～にもかかわらず, たとえ～でも
- [ ] **always** 副いつも, 常に
- [ ] **Amami Islands** 奄美諸島
- [ ] **America** 名アメリカ《国名・大陸》
- [ ] **American** 形アメリカ(人)の 名アメリカ人
- [ ] **among** 前(3つ以上のもの)の間で[に], ～の中で[に]
- [ ] **amount** 名①量, 額 ②《the –》合計 動(総計～に)なる
- [ ] **an** 冠①1つの, 1人の, ある ②～につき
- [ ] **ancestor** 名①祖先, 先祖 ②先人
- **Ancestors at the New Year** 死者の正月《沖縄の方言でジュールクニチという》
- [ ] **ancient** 形昔の, 古代の
- [ ] **and** 接①そして, ～と… ②《同じ語を結んで》ますます ③《結果を表して》それで, だから **again and again** 何度も繰り返して **and so** そこで, それだから **between A and B** A と B の間に **both A and B** A も B も
- [ ] **animal** 名動物 形動物の
- [ ] **annex** 動(武力などの)併合する
- [ ] **another** 形①もう1つ[1人]の ②別の 代①もう1つ[1人] ②別のもの
- [ ] **anticyclone** 名高気圧
- [ ] **any** 形①《疑問文で》何か, いくつかの ②《否定文で》何も, 少しも(～ない) ③《肯定文で》どの—も 代①《疑問文で》(～のうち)何か, どれか, 誰か ②《否定文で》少しも, 何も[誰も]～ない ③《肯定文で》どれも, 誰でも
- [ ] **anything** 代①《疑問文で》何か, どれでも ②《否定文で》何も, どれも(～ない) ③《肯定文で》何でも, どれでも **anything else** ほかの何か 副いくらか
- [ ] **anywhere** 副どこかへ[に], どこにも, どこへも, どこにでも
- [ ] **appear** 動現れる, 見えてくる
- [ ] **appoint** 動任命する, 指名する
- [ ] **approved** 動 approve (賛成する)の過去, 過去分詞
- [ ] **April** 名4月
- [ ] **archaeologist** 名考古学者
- [ ] **are** 動～である, (～に)いる[ある]《主語が you, we, they または複数名詞のときの be の現在形》

A

B
C
D
E
F
G
H
I
J
K
L
M
N
O
P
Q
R
S
T
U
V
W
X
Y
Z

□ **area** 名①地域, 地方, 区域, 場所 ②面積

□ **army** 名軍隊, 《the－》陸軍

□ **arose** 動arise（起こる）の過去

□ **around** 副①まわりに, あちこちに ②およそ, 約 go around 動き回る, あちらこちらに行く move around あちこち移動する walk around 歩き回る, ぶらぶら歩く 前①～のまわりに, ～のあちこちに

□ **as** 接①《as～as …の形で》…と同じくらい～ ②～のとおりに, ～のように ③～しながら, ～しているときに ④～するにつれて, ～にしたがって ⑤～なので ⑥～だけれども ⑦～する限りでは 前①～として（の）②～の時 副同じくらい 代①～のような ②～だが

□ **asa** 名アーサ《沖縄地方の方言で, ヒトエグサやアオサ等の緑藻類のこと》

□ **Asia** 名アジア

□ **Asian** 名アジア人 形アジアの

□ **aside** 副わきへ（に）, 離れて

□ **at** 前①《場所・時》～に［で］②《目標・方向》～に［を］, ～に向かって ③《原因・理由》～を見て［聞いて・知って］④～に従事して, ～の状態で at first 最初は, 初めのうちは at least 少なくとも at that time その時 at times 時には

□ **Atlas of the World's Languages in Danger** 消滅の危機にある世界の言語地図《ユネスコが発行している》

□ **attack** 動襲う, 攻める

□ **attend** 動①出席する ②世話をする, 仕える

□ **August** 名8月

□ **average** 名平均（値）, 並み 形平均の, 普通の 動平均して～になる

□ **avoid** 動避ける, （～を）しないようにする

□ **awamori** 名泡盛《タイ米を発酵・蒸留して作られる沖縄地方のお酒》

□ **away** 副離れて, 遠くに, 去って, わきに keep away 近づけない wash away 押し流す 形離れた, 遠征した

□ **ax** 名おの

B

□ **B.C.** 紀元前, 紀元前～年（＝Before Christ）

□ **back** 名①背中 ②裏, 後ろ 副①戻って ②後ろへ［に］called back to《be－》～に呼び戻される 形裏の, 後ろの 動後ろへ動く, 後退する

□ **bad** 形①悪い, へたな, まずい ②気の毒な ③（程度が）ひどい, 激しい

□ **bag** 名袋, かばん

□ **balance** 名均衡, 平均, 落ち着き 動釣り合いをとる

□ **ban** 名禁止, 禁制 動禁止する

□ **banana** 名バナナ

□ **banking** 動bank（取引する）の現在分詞 名銀行業

□ **base** 名基礎, 土台, 本部 military base 軍事基地 動《－on～》～に基礎を置く, 基づく

□ **baseball** 名野球

□ **based on** 《be－》～に基づく

□ **basketball** 名バスケットボール

□ **battle** 名戦闘, 戦い 動戦う

□ **be** 動～である, （～に）いる［ある］, ～となる 助①《現在分詞とともに用いて》～している ②《過去分詞とともに用いて》～される, ～されている

□ **beach** 名海辺, 浜

□ **beachhead** 名《軍事》上陸拠点, 海岸堡

□ **bead** 数珠玉, 《-s》ビーズ［のネックレス］

□ **beautiful** 形美しい, すばらしい

□ **beauty** 名①美, 美しい人［物］②

《the −》美点

□ **became** 動 become（なる）の過去

□ **because** 接（なぜなら）〜だから、〜という理由［原因］で **because of** 〜のために、〜の理由で

□ **become** 動 ①（〜に）なる ②（〜に）似合う ③become の過去分詞

□ **been** 動 be（〜である）の過去分詞 助 be（〜している・〜される）の過去分詞

□ **beer** 名 ビール

□ **before** 前 〜の前に［で］、〜より以前に **before long** やがて、まもなく 接 〜する前に 副 以前に

□ **began** 動 begin（始まる）の過去

□ **beginning** 動 begin（始まる）の現在分詞 名 初め、始まり

□ **begun** 動 begin（始まる）の過去分詞

□ **being** 動 be（〜である）の現在分詞 名 存在、生命、人間

□ **believe** 動 信じる、信じている、（〜と）思う、考える **believe in** 〜を信じる

□ **bell** 名 ベル、鈴、鐘

□ **beside** 前 ①〜のそばに、〜と並んで ②〜と比べると ③〜とはずれて

□ **best-known** 形 最もよく知られた

□ **better** 形 ①よりよい ②（人が）回復して 副 ①よりよく、より上手に ②むしろ

□ **between** 前（2つのもの）の間に［で・の］ **between A and B** A と B の間に 副 間に

□ **beyond** 前 〜を越えて、〜の向こうに 副 向こうに

□ **big** 形 ①大きい ②偉い、重要な 副 ①大きく、大いに ②自慢して

□ **bingata** 名 紅型《沖縄を代表する伝統的な染色技法》

□ **birth** 名 出産、誕生 **birth rate** 出生率

□ **bitter** 形 ①にがい ②つらい

□ **black** 形 黒い、有色の 名 黒、黒色

□ **bleaching** 名 漂白 **coral bleaching** サンゴの白化現象

□ **blend** 名 混合物

□ **blow** 動（風が）吹く、（風が）〜を吹き飛ばす

□ **blue** 形 青い 名 青（色）

□ **boat** 名 ボート、小舟、船

□ **body** 名 体、本体、胴体

□ **bombing** 名 爆撃、爆破

□ **bond** 名 縛るもの、結びつき、結束

□ **boost** 名 ①後押し、応援、励まし ②値上げ 動 ①押し上げる ②後援する、後援する ③（値段を）つり上げる

□ **born** 動 **be born** 生まれる 形 生まれた、生まれながらの

□ **both** 形 両方の、2つともの 副《both 〜 and …の形で》〜も…も両方とも 代 両方、両者、双方

□ **bottle** 名 瓶、ボトル 動 瓶に入れる［詰める］

□ **bottom** 名 底、下部、すそ野、ふもと 形 底の、底辺の

□ **bow** 動（〜に）お辞儀する 名 お辞儀、えしゃく

□ **box** 名 箱、容器

□ **branch** 名 ①枝 ②支流、支部 動 枝を広げる、枝分かれする

□ **brand** 名 ブランド、商標、品種

□ **Brazil** 名 ブラジル《国》

□ **break** 動 壊す、折る **break up** ばらばらになる、解散させる

□ **brewery** 名 ［ビールなどの］醸造所

□ **bridge** 名 橋 動 橋をかける

□ **brief** 形 ①短い時間の ②簡単な 名 要点、概要

□ **bright** 形 輝いている、鮮明な

□ **brilliantly** 副 きらきらと、見事に

- □ **bring** 動①持ってくる, 連れてくる ②もたらす, 生じる
- □ **brought** 動 bring (持ってくる)の過去, 過去分詞
- □ **brown** 形茶色の
- □ **bubble** 名泡
- □ **build** 動建てる, 確立する 名体格, 構造
- □ **build-up** 名積み上げ, 積み重ね
- □ **building** 動 build (建てる)の現在分詞 名建物, 建造物, ビルディング
- □ **built** 動 build (建てる)の過去, 過去分詞
- □ **bulldozer** 名ブルドーザー
- □ **bullet** 名銃弾, 弾丸状のもの
- □ **burden** 名①荷 ②重荷 動荷[負担]を負わす
- □ **business** 名①職業, 仕事 ②商売 形①職業の ②商売上の
- □ **bustle** 動①忙しく[せかせか]動く ②せき立てる 名せわしげな動き
- □ **but** 接①でも, しかし ②〜を除いて not only 〜 but (also) …〜だけでなく…もまた 前〜を除いて, 〜のほかは 副ただ, のみ, ほんの
- □ **by** 前①《位置》〜のそばに[で] ②《手段・方法・行為者・基準》〜によって, 〜で ③《期限》〜までには ④《通過・経由》〜を経由して, 〜を通って by then その時までに followed by その後に〜が続いて pass by 〜のそばを通る[通り過ぎる] 副そばに, 通り過ぎて

C

- □ **cake** 名①菓子, ケーキ ②固まり rice cake 餅
- □ **calendar** 名カレンダー, 暦
- □ **call** 動①呼ぶ, 叫ぶ ②電話をかける ③立ち寄る 名①呼び声, 叫び ②電話(をかけること) ③短い訪問

- □ **called back to** 《be –》〜に呼び戻される
- □ **calling** 動 call (呼ぶ)の現在分詞 名①呼ぶこと ②召集, 呼び出し ③天職, 職業
- □ **came** 動 come (来る)の過去
- □ **camp** 名野営(地), キャンプ 動野営する, キャンプする
- □ **can** 助①〜できる ②〜してもよい ③〜でありうる ④《否定文で》〜のはずがない
- □ **canoe** 名カヌー
- □ **Cape Maeda** 真栄田岬
- □ **Cape Manzamo** 万座毛《沖縄海岸国定公園にも指定されている景勝地》
- □ **car** 名自動車, (列車の)車両
- □ **care** 名①心配, 注意 ②世話, 介護 take care 気をつける, 注意する
- □ **carry** 動①運ぶ, 連れていく, 持ち歩く ②伝わる, 伝える carry on 続ける, 継承する
- □ **carve** 動彫る, 彫刻する
- □ **case** 名①事件, 問題, 事柄 ②実例, 場合 ③実状, 状況
- □ **castle** 名城, 大邸宅
- □ **catch** 動①つかまえる ②追いつく 名つかまえること, 捕球
- □ **cause** 名①原因, 理由, 動機 ②大義, 主張 動 (〜の)原因となる, 引き起こす
- □ **cave** 名洞穴, 洞窟
- □ **celebrate** 動①祝う, 祝福する ②祝典を開く
- □ **celebrated** 動 celebrate (祝う)の過去, 過去分詞 形名高い, 有名な
- □ **celebration** 名①祝賀 ②祝典, 儀式
- □ **center** 名①中心, 中央 ②中心地 [人物] 動集中する[させる]
- □ **central** 形中央の, 主要な
- □ **century** 名100年間, 1世紀

- [ ] **ceramic** 名 ①《通例-s》陶磁器 ②陶芸
- [ ] **ceremony** 名 儀式, 式典
- [ ] **certainly** 副 確かに, 必ず
- [ ] **chance** 名 ①偶然, 運 ②好機 ③見込み
- [ ] **change** 動 ①変わる, 変える ②交換する 名 ①変化, 変更 ②取り替え, 乗り換え
- [ ] **character** 名 ①特性, 個性 ②文字, 記号
- [ ] **charm** 名 魅力, 魔力
- [ ] **chase** 動 ①追跡する, 追い[探し]求める ②追い立てる
- [ ] **check** 動 照合する, 検査する
- [ ] **children** 名 child（子ども）の複数
- [ ] **chimney** 名 煙突（状のもの）
- [ ] **China** 名 ①中国《国名》 ②《c-》陶磁器, 瀬戸物
- [ ] **Chinese** 形 中国（人）の 名 ①中国人 ②中国語
- [ ] **Chinese-style** 形 中国風の
- [ ] **Chinese martial arts** 中国武術
- [ ] **choice** 名 選択（の範囲・自由）, えり好み
- [ ] **choose** 動 選ぶ, （～に）決める
- [ ] **chose** 動 choose（選ぶ）の過去
- [ ] **chosen** 動 choose（選ぶ）の過去分詞 形 選ばれた, 精選された
- [ ] **churaumi** 美ら海《沖縄の方言で「美しい海」を指す》
- [ ] **circle** 名 円, 円周, 輪 in a circle 輪になって
- [ ] **city** 名 ①都市, 都会 ②《the – 》(全)市民
- [ ] **civil** 形 ①一般人の, 民間（人）の ②国内の, 国家の
- [ ] **civilization** 名 文明
- [ ] **clan** 名 ①氏族 ②一家, 一門
- [ ] **classic** 形 古典的の, 伝統的な 名 古典
- [ ] **clay** 名 粘土, 白土
- [ ] **clear** 形 ①はっきりした, 明白な ②澄んだ
- [ ] **climate** 名 気候, 風土, 環境
- [ ] **close** 形 ①近い ②親しい ③狭い 副 ①接近して ②密集して 動 ①閉まる, 閉める ②終える, 閉店する
- [ ] **closed** 動 close（閉まる）の過去, 過去分詞 形 閉じた
- [ ] **closeness** 名 〔距離の〕近さ, 〔関係の〕親密さ
- [ ] **cloth** 名 布（地）, テーブルクロス, ふきん
- [ ] **coast** 名 海岸, 沿岸
- [ ] **coastline** 名 海岸線
- [ ] **cocktail** 名 カクテル
- [ ] **coffin** 名 棺
- [ ] **coin** 名 硬貨, コイン
- [ ] **cola** 名 コーラ《炭酸飲料》
- [ ] **color** 名 色, 色彩 動 色をつける
- [ ] **colored** 動 color（色をつける）の過去, 過去分詞 形 色のついた
- [ ] **colorful** 形 ①カラフルな, 派手な ②生き生きとした
- [ ] **coloring** 名 着色, 彩色
- [ ] **combine** 動 ①結合する[させる] ②連合する, 協力する 名 合同, 連合
- [ ] **come** 動 ①来る, 行く, 現れる ②(出来事が)起こる, 生じる ③～になる ④comeの過去分詞 come about 起こる come across ～を渡って来る come into ～に入ってくる
- [ ] **coming** 動 come（来る）の現在分詞 形 今度の, 来たるべき 名 到来, 来ること
- [ ] **commodore** 名 海軍准将, 提督
- [ ] **common** 形 ①共通の, 共同の ②普通の, 平凡な ③一般の, 公共の
- [ ] **communicate** 動 ①知らせる, 連絡する ②理解し合う

□ **community** 图 ①団体, 共同社会, 地域社会 ②《the –》社会 (一般), 世間 ③共有, 共同責任

□ **company** 图 ①会社 ②交際, 同席 ③友だち, 仲間, 一団, 人の集まり

□ **compare** 動 ①比較する, 対照する ②たとえる

□ **compared to** 《be –》~と比較して, ~に比べれば

□ **competition** 图 競争, 競合, コンペ

□ **complete** 圏 完全な, まったくの, 完成した 動 完成させる

□ **completely** 圏 完全に, すっかり

□ **concept** 图 ①概念, 観念, テーマ ②(計画案などの) 基本的な方向

□ **concrete** 圏 ①コンクリート (製) の ②具体的な, 明確な 图 コンクリート

□ **condition** 图 ①(健康) 状態, 境遇 ②《-s》状況, 様子 ③条件

□ **connect** 動 つながる, つなぐ, 関係づける

□ **connected** 動 connect (つながる) の過去, 過去分詞 圏 結合した, 関係のある

□ **connection** 图 ①つながり, 関係 ②縁故

□ **consider** 動 ①考慮する, ~しようと思う ②(~と) みなす

□ **contain** 動 ①含む, 入っている ②(感情などを) 抑える

□ **continent** 图 ①大陸, 陸地 ②《the C-》ヨーロッパ大陸

□ **continue** 動 続く, 続ける, (中断後) 再開する, (ある方向に) 移動していく

□ **control** 動 ①管理 [支配] する ②抑制する, コントロールする 图 ①管理, 支配 (力) ②抑制

□ **conquer** 動 征服する, 制圧する

□ **conveniently** 圏 好都合なことに, 便利なことに

□ **cooking** 動 cook (料理する) の過去, 過去分詞 图 料理 (法), クッキング cooking fire いろり

□ **coral** 图 サンゴ (珊瑚) coral bleaching サンゴの白化現象 圏 サンゴの

□ **core** 图 核心, 中心, 芯

□ **corner** 图 ①曲がり角, 角 ②すみ, はずれ

□ **corps** 图 軍団, 部隊 Marine Corps アメリカ海兵隊

□ **cost** 图 ①値段, 費用 ②損失, 犠牲 動 (金・費用が) かかる, (~を) 要する, (人に金額を) 費やさせる

□ **costume** 图 衣装, 服装

□ **cotton** 图 ①綿, 綿花 ②綿織物, 綿糸

□ **could** 動 ①can (~できる) の過去 ②《控え目な推量・可能性・願望などを表す》

□ **country** 图 ①国 ②《the –》田舎, 郊外 ③地域, 領域, 分野

□ **course** 图 of course もちろん, 当然

□ **court** 图 ①中庭, コート ②法廷, 裁判所 ③宮廷, 宮殿

□ **cover** 動 ①覆う, 包む, 隠す ②扱う, (~に) わたる, 及ぶ

□ **cow** 图 雌牛, 乳牛

□ **cowrie** 图 《貝》コヤスガイ

□ **craft** 图 技術, 技巧

□ **crash** 图 ①激突, 墜落 ②(壊れるときの) すさまじい音

□ **create** 動 創造する, 生み出す, 引き起こす

□ **creative** 圏 創造力のある, 独創的な

□ **creature** 图 (神の) 創造物, 生物, 動物

□ **crime** 图 ①(法律上の) 罪, 犯罪 ②悪事, よくない行為

□ **crop** 图 作物, 収穫 動 収穫する, 刈

り込む

- □ **cruise** 名〔船旅の〕クルージング

- □ **cultural** 形文化の, 文化的な
Important Cultural Properties 重要文化財

- □ **culture** 名①文化 ②教養 ③耕作, 栽培 動耕す, 栽培する

- □ **cup** 名カップ, 茶わん

- □ **currency** 名①通貨, 貨幣 ②流通, 通用すること

- □ **current** 名流れ, 電流, 風潮

- □ **custom** 名習慣, 慣例, 風俗

- □ **cut down** 切り倒す, 打ちのめす

- □ **cutting** 動cut (切る)の現在分詞

- □ **cycle** 名周期, 循環

D

- □ **daily** 形毎日の, 日常の 副毎日, 日ごとに

- □ **damage** 名損害, 損傷 動損害を与える, 損なう

- □ **dance** 動踊る, ダンスをする 名ダンス, ダンスパーティー

- □ **dancer** 名踊り子, ダンサー

- □ **danger** 名危険, 障害, 脅威

- □ **date** 名日付, 年月日 動日付を記す

- □ **day** 名①日中, 昼間 ②日, 期日 ③《-s》時代, 生涯 **New Year's Day** 元日 **these days** このごろ

- □ **death** 名①死, 死ぬこと ②《the –》終えん, 消滅

- □ **decorate** 動飾る

- □ **deep** 形①深い, 深さ～の ②深遠な ③濃い

- □ **definitely** 副①限定的に, 明確に, 確実に ②まったくそのとおり

- □ **degree** 名①程度, 階級, 位, 身分 ②(温度・角度の) 度

- □ **deigo** 名デイゴ《沖縄の県花》

- □ **deny** 動否定する, 断る, 受けつけない

- □ **depression** 名不景気, 不況 **Great Depression**《the –》世界大恐慌 (1929年10月28–29日)

- □ **describe** 動 (言葉で) 描写する, 特色を述べる, 説明する

- □ **designated** 形指定 [指名] された

- □ **destroy** 動破壊する, 絶滅させる, 無効にする

- □ **develop** 動①発達する [させる] ②開発する

- □ **development** 名①発達, 発展 ②開発

- □ **dialect** 名方言, なまり

- □ **dialogue** 名対話, 話し合い

- □ **diamond** 名①ダイヤモンド ②ひし形

- □ **did** 動do (～をする)の過去 助do の過去

- □ **die** 動死ぬ, 消滅する

- □ **differ** 動異なる, 違う, 意見が合わない

- □ **difference** 名違い, 相違, 差

- □ **different** 形異なった, 違った, 別の, さまざまな

- □ **differently** 副 (～と) 異なって, 違って

- □ **dining** 動dine (食事をする)の現在分詞 名食事, 夕食をとること

- □ **direct** 形まっすぐな, 直接の, 率直な

- □ **direction** 名①方向, 方角 ②指導, 指揮

- □ **disability** 名①無力 ②身体障害

- □ **disappear** 動見えなくなる, 姿を消す, なくなる

- □ **dish** 名①大皿 ②料理

- □ **display** 動展示する, 示す 名展示, 陳列, 表出

- □ **distill** 動蒸留する

□ **diverse** 形 ①種々の, 多様な ②異なった

□ **divide** 動分かれる, 分ける, 割れる, 割る **divide into** ～に分かれる

□ **divided into** 《be－》分けられる

□ **diving** 名潜水, ダイビング

□ **do** 助①《ほかの動詞とともに用いて現在形の否定文・疑問文をつくる》②《同じ動詞を繰り返す代わりに用いる》③《動詞を強調するのに用いる》動～をする **plan to do** ～するつもりである

□ **Do-Re-Mi** ドレミ《音階の音名》

□ **does** 動do（～をする）の3人称単数現在 助doの3人称単数現在

□ **doing** 熟start doing ～し始める

□ **dollar** 名①ドル《米国などの通貨単位》②《-s》金銭

□ **domain** 名統治地域, 領土 **Satsuma Domain** 薩摩藩

□ **done** 動do（～をする）の過去分詞

□ **door** 名①ドア, 戸 ②一軒, 一戸

□ **doorway** 名戸口, 玄関, 出入り口

□ **double** 形①2倍の, 二重の ②対の

□ **down** 副①下へ, 降りて, 低くなって ②倒れて **cut down** 切り倒す, 打ちのめす **pass down**（次の世代に）伝える **write down** 書き留める 前～の下方へ, ～を下って 形下方の, 下りの

□ **dragon fruit** ドラゴンフルーツ, 火龍果

□ **drawn** 動draw（引く）の過去分詞

□ **dress** 名ドレス, 衣服, 正装 動①服を着る［着せる］②飾る

□ **drier** 名乾燥機,（ヘア）ドライヤー

□ **drink** 動飲む, 飲酒する 名飲み物, 酒, 1杯

□ **drinker** 名酒飲み, 家畜用の給水機

□ **drinking** 動drink（飲む）の現在分詞 名飲むこと, 飲酒

□ **drive** 動車で行く,（車を）運転する

□ **drum** 名太鼓, ドラム 動太鼓を鳴らす, ドラムを打つ

□ **due** 形予定された, 期日のきている, 支払われるべき **due to** ～によって, ～が原因で 名当然の権利

□ **during** 前～の間（ずっと）

□ **dwelling** 名住居, 居住

□ **dye** 動染める, 染まる 名染料

□ **dyeing** 名染色

□ **dynamic** 形活動的な, 動的な, ダイナミックな

□ **dynasty** 名王朝［王家］（の統治期間）

E

□ **each** 形それぞれの, 各自の 代それぞれ, 各自 副それぞれに **each other** お互いに **each time** ～するたびに

□ **ear** 名耳, 聴覚

□ **early** 形①（時間や時期が）早い ②初期の, 幼少の, 若い 副①早く, 早めに ②初期に, 初めのころに

□ **east** 名《the－》東, 東部, 東方 形東の, 東方［東部］の

□ **East China Sea** 東シナ海

□ **easy** 形①やさしい, 簡単な ②気楽な, くつろいだ

□ **eat** 動食べる, 食事する

□ **eaten** 動eat（食べる）の過去分詞

□ **economic** 形経済学の, 経済上の

□ **economically** 副経済的に, 節約して

□ **economy** 名①経済, 財政 ②節約

□ **ecosystem** 名生態系

□ **Edo** 名江戸《地名》

□ **education** 名教育, 教養

□ **effect** 名①影響, 効果, 結果 ②実施,

発効 動もたらす, 達成する
- **effort** 名努力(の成果)
- **eight** 名8(の数字), 8人[個] 形8の, 8人[個]の
- **Eisa** 名エイサー《沖縄でお盆の時期に踊られる伝統芸能》
- **electricity** 名電気
- **elementary** 形①初歩の ②単純な, 簡単な
- **else** 副①そのほかに[の], 代わりに ②さもないと **anything else** ほかの何か
- **embassy** 名大使館
- **emotion** 名感激, 感動, 感情
- **enable** 動(〜することを)可能にする, 容易にする
- **end** 名①終わり, 終末, 死 ②果て, 末, 端 ③目的 **put an end to** 〜に終止符を打つ, 〜を終わらせる, 〜に決着をつける 動終わる, 終える
- **endangered** 動endanger(危険にさらす)の過去, 過去分詞 形危険にさらされた
- **enjoy** 動楽しむ, 享受する
- **enter** 動①入る ②(考えなどが)(心・頭に)浮かぶ
- **entertain** 動①もてなす, 接待する ②楽しませる
- **entire** 形全体の, 完全な, まったくの
- **entrance** 名①入り口, 入場 ②開始
- **environment** 名①環境 ②周囲(の状況), 情勢
- **environmental** 形①環境の, 周囲の ②環境保護の
- **envoy** 名使節, 使者, 外交使節
- **era** 名時代, 年代
- **erase** 動①消える ②消去する, 抹消する
- **escape** 動逃げる, 免れる, もれる 名逃亡, 脱出, もれ

- **etiquette** 名エチケット, 礼儀(作法)
- **Europe** 名ヨーロッパ
- **even** 副①《強意》〜でさえも, 〜ですら, いっそう, なおさら ②平等に **even though** 〜であるけれども, 〜にもかかわらず 形①平らな, 水平の ②等しい, 均一の ③落ち着いた 動平らになる[する], 釣り合いをとる
- **event** 名出来事, 事件, イベント
- **eventually** 副結局は
- **every** 形①どの〜も, すべての, あらゆる ②毎〜, 〜ごとの
- **everyone** 代誰でも, 皆
- **everything** 代すべてのこと[もの], 何でも, 何もかも
- **evidence** 名①証拠, 証人 ②形跡
- **evil** 形①邪悪な ②有害な, 不吉な 名①邪悪 ②害, わざわい, 不幸
- **example** 名例, 見本, 模範 **for example** たとえば
- **excellent** 形優れた, 優秀な
- **except** 前〜を除いて, 〜のほかは 接〜ということを除いて
- **exception** 名例外, 除外, 異論
- **exclusively** 副①排他的に, 独占的に ②もっぱら
- **exist** 動存在する, 生存する, ある, いる
- **expand** 動①広げる, 拡張[拡大]する ②発展させる, 拡充する
- **experience** 動経験[体験]する
- **export** 動輸出する 名輸出, 国外への持ち出し

F

- **fabric** 名①織物, 生地 ②構造
- **facility** 名①《-ties》施設, 設備 ②器用さ, 容易さ
- **fact** 名事実, 真相 **in fact** つまり,

実は, 要するに

- [ ] **fair** 形 正しい, 公平[正当]な

- [ ] **fake** 動 ~をでっち上げる, ~のふりをする, [仮病を]使う

- [ ] **fall** 動 ①落ちる, 倒れる ②(値段・温度が)下がる ③(ある状態に)急に陥る **fall on** [日付が]~に当たる 名 ①落下, 墜落 ②崩壊

- [ ] **family** 名 家族, 家庭, 一門, 家柄

- [ ] **famous** 形 有名な, 名高い

- [ ] **fan** 名 ①愛好者 ②扇(状のもの), うちわ

- [ ] **far** 副 ①遠くに, はるかに, 離れて ②(比較級を強めて)ずっと, はるかに **far from** ~から遠い, ~どころか 形 遠い, 向こうの

- [ ] **farm** 名 農場, 農家 動 (~を)耕作する

- [ ] **Far East** 極東

- [ ] **farmer** 名 農民, 農場経営者

- [ ] **farming** 動 farm (耕作する)の現在分詞 名 農業, 農作業

- [ ] **fast** 形 (速度が)速い 副 速く, 急いで

- [ ] **fate** 名 ①《時に F-》運命, 宿命 ②破滅, 悲運 動 (~の)運命にある

- [ ] **FC Ryukyu** FC琉球《沖縄のプロサッカーチーム》

- [ ] **feast** 名 ①饗宴, ごちそう ②(宗教上の)祝祭日 ③大きな楽しみ

- [ ] **feature** 名 特徴, 特色

- [ ] **feel** 動 感じる, (~と)思う

- [ ] **feeling** 動 feel (感じる)の現在分詞 名 感じ, 気持ち

- [ ] **fell** 動 fall (落ちる)の過去

- [ ] **felt** 動 feel (感じる)の過去, 過去分詞

- [ ] **female** 形 女性の, 婦人の, 雌の 名 婦人, 雌

- [ ] **fence** 名 囲み, さく 動 さくをめぐらす, 防御する

- [ ] **ferment** 動 発酵させる

- [ ] **ferry** 名 渡し場, フェリーボート

- [ ] **festival** 名 祭り, 祝日, ~祭

- [ ] **few** 形 ①ほとんどない, 少数の(~しかない) ②《a-》少数の, 少しはある 代 少数の人[物]

- [ ] **fiber** 名 繊維, 食物繊維, 繊維質

- [ ] **field** 名 野原, 田畑

- [ ] **fierce** 形 どう猛な, 荒々しい, すさまじい, 猛烈な

- [ ] **fifteenth** 名 第15番目(の人[物]), 15日 形 第15番目の

- [ ] **fight** 動 (~と)戦う, 争う

- [ ] **fighting** 名 戦闘

- [ ] **final** 形 最後の, 決定的な

- [ ] **finally** 副 最後に, ついに, 結局

- [ ] **finance** 名 ①財政, 財務 ②(銀行からの)資金, 融資 ③《-s》財政状態, 財源

- [ ] **find** 動 ①見つける ②(~と)わかる, 気づく, ~と考える ③得る

- [ ] **fine** 形 ①元気な ②美しい, りっぱな, 申し分ない, 結構な ③細かい, 微妙な

- [ ] **finish** 動 終わる, 終える 名 終わり, 最後

- [ ] **fire** 名 ①火, 炎, 火事 ②砲火, 攻撃 **cooking fire** いろり

- [ ] **firm** 形 堅い, しっかりした, 断固とした

- [ ] **first** 名 最初, 第一(の人・物) **at first** 最初は, 初めのうちは 形 ①第一の, 最初の ②最も重要な 副 第一に, 最初に

- [ ] **First Sho Dynasty** 《the-》第一尚氏王統《1406–69》

- [ ] **First Sino-Japanese War** 《the-》日清戦争

- [ ] **First World War** 《the-》第一次世界大戦

- [ ] **fish** 名 魚 動 釣りをする

- [ ] **fisherman** 名 漁師, (趣味の)釣り人

☐ **fishing** 動 fish（釣りをする）の現在分詞 名釣り, 魚業 形釣りの, 漁業の

☐ **fist** 名こぶし, げんこつ

☐ **five** 名5（の数字）, 5人［個］ 形5の, 5人［個］の

☐ **flame** 名炎,（炎のような）輝き 動燃え上がる,（顔などが）さっと赤らむ

☐ **flatten** 動①平らにする, 伸ばす ②ばったりと倒す

☐ **flavor** 名風味, 味わい, 趣 動風味を添える

☐ **flexible** 形（物が）曲がりやすい, しなやかな

☐ **flight** 名飛ぶこと, 飛行,（飛行機の）フライト

☐ **flow** 動流れ出る, 流れる, あふれる 名①流出 ②流ちょう（なこと）

☐ **flower** 名①花, 草花 ②満開 動花が咲く

☐ **fluffy** 形ふわふわした, 柔らかい

☐ **flying** 動 fly（飛ぶ）の現在分詞 名飛行 形飛んでいる, 空中に浮かぶ,（飛ぶように）速い

☐ **focus** 名①焦点, ピント ②関心の的, 着眼点 ③中心 動①焦点を合わせる ②（関心・注意を）集中させる

☐ **folk dance** 民族舞踊

☐ **folk song** 民謡

☐ **folkcraft** 名民芸

☐ **follow** 動①ついていく, あとをたどる ②（〜の）結果として起こる ③（忠告などに）従う **followed by** その後に〜が続いて

☐ **following** 形《the −》次の, 次に続く

☐ **food** 名食物, えさ, 肥料

☐ **for** 前①《目的・原因・対象》〜にとって, 〜のために［の］, 〜に対して ②《期間》〜間 ③《代理》〜の代わりに ④《方向》〜へ（向かって）**for example** たとえば **for 〜 years** 〜年間, 〜年にわたって 接というわけ

は〜, なぜなら〜, だから

☐ **force** 名力, 勢い 動①強制する, 力ずくで〜する, 余儀なく〜させる ②押しやる, 押し込む

☐ **forcefully** 副力強く

☐ **foreign** 形外国の, よその, 異質な

☐ **forest** 名森林

☐ **forestry** 名林業, 森林管理

☐ **form** 名①形, 形式 ②書式 動形づくる

☐ **formation** 名①形成, 編成 ②隊形, フォーメーション

☐ **fort** 名砦, 要塞

☐ **fought** 動 fight（戦う）の過去, 過去分詞

☐ **found** 動①find（見つける）の過去, 過去分詞 ②〜の基礎を築く, 〜を設立する

☐ **four** 名4（の数字）, 4人［個］ 形4の, 4人［個］の

☐ **fourth** 形第4の, 4番目の 名4番目（の物［人］）, 第4番, 4日 副第4に, 4番目に

☐ **free** 形自由な, 開放された, 自由に〜できる

☐ **French** 形フランス（人・語）の 名①フランス語 ②《the −》フランス人

☐ **fresh** 形新鮮な, 生気のある

☐ **from** 前①《出身・出発点・時間・順序・原料》〜から ②《原因・理由》〜がもとで **from 〜 to …** 〜から…まで

☐ **front** 名正面, 前 **in front of** 〜の前に, 〜の正面に 形正面の, 前面の

☐ **fruit** 名①果実, 実 ②《-s》成果, 利益 動実を結ぶ

☐ **fuchiba** 名フーチバー《沖縄の方言で「ヨモギ」を指す》

☐ **fugarasa** ふうがらさ《与那国島の方言で「ありがとう」》

☐ **fulfill** 動（義務・約束を）果たす,（要

求・条件を) 満たす

□ **full** 形 ①満ちた, いっぱいの, 満期の ②完全な, 盛りの, 充実した **be full of** 〜で一杯である 名 全部

□ **full-scale** 形 本格的な, 完全な, 全面的な

□ **further** 形 いっそう遠い, その上の, なおいっそうの 副 いっそう遠く, その上に, もっと

□ **Futenma** 名 普天間《沖縄県宜野湾市の地名》

□ **future** 名 未来, 将来 **in the future** 将来は 形 未来の, 将来の

G

□ **gain** 動 ①得る, 増す ②進歩する, 進む

□ **gajumaru tree** ガジュマル《沖縄から屋久島にかけて自生している樹木》

□ **game** 名 ゲーム, 試合, 遊び, 競技

□ **gap** 名 ギャップ, 隔たり, すき間 動 すき間ができる

□ **gate** 名 ①門, 扉, 入り口 ②(空港・駅などの) ゲート

□ **gather** 動 ①集まる, 集める ②生じる, 増す ③推測する

□ **gathering** 動 gather (集まる) の現在分詞 名 ①集まり, 集会 ②ひだ, ギャザー

□ **generation** 名 ①同世代の人々 ②一世代

□ **gentle** 形 ①優しい, 温和な ②柔らかな

□ **get** 動 ①得る, 手に入れる ②(ある状態に) なる, いたる ③わかる, 理解する ④〜させる, 〜を (…の状態に) する ⑤(ある場所に) 達する, 着く

□ **Ginowan** 名 宜野湾市《沖縄本島中部西海岸側》

□ **give** 動 ①与える, 贈る ②伝える, 述べる ③(〜を) する **give off** 発散

する, 放つ

□ **given** 動 give (与える) の過去分詞 形 与えられた

□ **glass** 名 ガラス (状のもの), コップ, グラス

□ **global** 形 地球 (上) の, 地球規模の, 世界的な, 国際的な

□ **global warming** 地球温暖化

□ **globe** 名 ①球 ②地球

□ **glow** 動 ①白熱, 輝き ②ほてり, 熱情

□ **go** 動 ①行く, 出かける ②動く ③進む, 経過する, いたる ④(ある状態に) なる **be going to** 〜するつもりである **go around** 動き回る, あちらこちらに行く **go into** 〜に入る, (仕事) に就く

□ **god** 名 神

□ **golden** 形 ①金色の ②金製の ③貴重な

□ **good** 形 ①よい, 上手な, 優れた, 美しい ②(数量・程度が) かなりの, 相当な 名 ①善, 徳, 益, 幸福 ②《-s》財産, 品, 物質

□ **goods** 名 ①商品, 品物 ②財産, 所有物

□ **govern** 動 治める, 管理する, 支配する

□ **government** 名 政治, 政府, 支配

□ **goya** 名 ゴーヤー《沖縄本島の方言で「ニガウリ」を指す》

□ **grab** 動 ①ふいにつかむ, ひったくる ②横取りする 名 ひっつかむこと, 横取り

□ **gradually** 副 だんだんと

□ **grain** 名 ①穀物, 穀類, (穀物の) 粒 ②粒, 極少量 動 粒にする

□ **grandchildren** 名 grandchild (孫) の複数

□ **grape** 名 ブドウ

□ **grave** 名 墓

□ **gravestone** 名 墓石

□ **gray** 形①灰色の ②どんよりした, 憂うつな 名灰色

□ **great** 形①大きい, 広大な, (量や程度が)たいへんな ②偉大な, 優れた ③すばらしい, おもしろい Great Depression《the－》世界大恐慌 (1929年10月28–29日)

□ **greatly** 副大いに

□ **Greek** 形ギリシア(人・語)の 名①ギリシア人 ②ギリシア語

□ **green** 名①緑色 ②草地, 芝生, 野菜

□ **greet** 動①あいさつする ②(喜んで)迎える

□ **grew** 動 grow (成長する)の過去

□ **ground** 名地面, 土, 土地 動①基づかせる ②着陸する ③grind (ひく)の過去, 過去分詞

□ **group** 名集団, 群 動集まる

□ **grow** 動①成長する, 育つ, 育てる ②増大する, 大きくなる, (次第に～に)なる grow into 成長して～になる

□ **growing** 動 grow (成長する)の現在分詞 形成長期にある, 大きくなりつつある

□ **grown** 動 grow (成長する)の過去分詞 形成長した, 成人した

□ **growth** 名成長, 発展 形成長している

□ **guard** 名①警戒, 見張り ②番人 動番をする, 監視する, 守る

□ **guardian** 名守護神

□ **guest** 名客, ゲスト

□ **gurukun** 名グルクン《沖縄の県魚で「タカサゴ」のこと》

□ **gusuku** 名グスク《沖縄の方言で「城」「城砦」を指す》

□ **Gusuku period** 《the－》グスク時代

□ **Gusuku Sites and Related Properties of the Kingdom of Ryukyu** 《the－》琉球王国のグ

スク及び関連遺産群

H

□ **Haaree** 名ハーレー《ハーリーの糸満での呼び名》

□ **Haarii** 名ハーリー《毎年旧暦の5月4日に沖縄県各地の漁港で行われる船競漕とその祭り》

□ **had** 動 have (持つ)の過去, 過去分詞 助 have の過去《過去完了の文をつくる》

□ **half** 名半分

□ **hanaori** 名花織《沖縄の伝統的紋織の一つ》

□ **hand** 動手渡す

□ **happen** 動①(出来事が)起こる, 生じる ②偶然[たまたま]～する

□ **happening** 動 happen (起こる)の現在分詞 名出来事, 事件

□ **happiness** 名幸せ, 喜び

□ **hard** 副①一生懸命に ②激しく ③堅く work hard 一生懸命に[せっせと]働く

□ **harden** 動固める, 固くする, 頑固にする

□ **hardship** 名(耐えがたい)苦難, 辛苦

□ **harm** 名害, 損害, 危害 動傷つける, 損なう

□ **harsh** 形厳しい, とげとげしい, 不快な

□ **harvest** 名①収穫(物), 刈り入れ ②成果, 報い 動収穫する

□ **Haryu Sen** 爬竜船《沖縄のハーリーで用いられる船》

□ **has** 動 have (持つ)の3人称単数現在 助 have の3人称単数現在《現在完了の文をつくる》

□ **Hatenohama Beach** はての浜《久米島沖東5kmに浮かぶ砂だけからなる3つの無人島の総称》

□ **Hateruma Island** 波照間島《沖縄県の八重山列島にある日本最南端の有人島》

□ **have** 動①持つ, 持っている, 抱く ②(~が) ある, いる ③食べる, 飲む ④経験する,(病気に)かかる ⑤催す, 開く ⑥(人に)~させる **have to ~** しなければならない 助《〈have + 過去分詞〉の形で現在完了の文をつくる》~した, ~したことがある, ずっと~している

□ **Hawaii** 名ハワイ《米国の州》

□ **he** 代彼は[が]

□ **health** 名健康(状態), 衛生, 保健

□ **healthy** 形健康な, 健全な, 健康によい

□ **heap** 名(積み重ねた)山, かたまり 動積み上げる, 重ねる

□ **hearing** 動hear (聞く) の現在分詞 名聞くこと, 聴取, 聴力

□ **heat** 名①熱, 暑さ ②熱気, 熱意, 激情 動熱する, 暖める

□ **held** 動hold (つかむ) の過去, 過去分詞 **held in**《be ~》(場所など)で開催される **held on**《be ~》(日付・年など)に開催される

□ **hell** 名地獄, 地獄のようなところ[状態]

□ **help** 動①助ける, 手伝う ②給仕する 名助け, 手伝い

□ **helping** 動help (助ける) の現在分詞 名助力, 手助け 形救いの, 助けの

□ **heritage** 名遺産 **World Heritage Site** 世界遺産

□ **hibiscus** 名《植物》ハイビスカス

□ **hide** 動隠す,〔人を〕かくまう, 秘密にする

□ **high** 形①高い ②気高い, 高価な 副①高く ②ぜいたくに 名高い所

□ **hill** 名丘, 塚

□ **him** 代彼を[に]

□ **Himeyuri Memorial Tower** ひめゆりの塔《沖縄戦末期に沖縄陸軍病院第三外科が置かれた壕の跡に立つ慰霊碑》

□ **himself** 代彼自身

□ **Hinukan** 名ヒヌカン《沖縄で信仰される火の神》

□ **his** 代①彼の ②彼のもの

□ **historic** 形歴史上有名[重要]な, 歴史的な

□ **history** 名歴史, 経歴

□ **hold** 動①つかむ, 持つ, 抱く ②保つ, 持ちこたえる ③(会などを)開く 名①つかむこと, 保有 ②支配[理解]力

□ **holy** 形聖なる, 神聖な

□ **home** 名家, 自国, 故郷, 家庭 副家に, 自国へ 形家の, 家庭の, 地元の

□ **Honshu** 名本州

□ **hope** 動望む, (~であるようにと)思う

□ **horror** 名①恐怖, ぞっとすること ②嫌悪

□ **host** 動~を主催する, ~で主人役を務める

□ **hot** 形暑い, 熱い

□ **hotel** 名ホテル, 旅館

□ **hour** 名1時間, 時間

□ **house** 名①家, 家庭 ②(特定の目的のための)建物, 小屋

□ **how** 副①どうやって, どれくらい, どんなふうに ②なんて (~だろう) ③《関係副詞》~する方法

□ **however** 副たとえ~でも 接けれども, だが

□ **human** 形人間の, 人の 名人間

□ **humanity** 名人間性, 人間らしさ

□ **hundred** 名①100 (の数字), 100人[個] ②《-s》何百, 多数 形①100の, 100人[個]の ②多数の

□ **hunt** 動狩る, 狩りをする, 探し求める 名狩り, 追跡

□ **hunting** 動hunt (狩る) の現在分

詞 名狩り, 狩猟, ハンティング, 捜索
- □ **hut** 名簡易住居, あばら屋, 山小屋

I

- □ **ice** 名①氷 ②氷菓子 動凍る, 凍らす, 氷で冷やす
- □ **idea** 名考え, 意見, アイデア, 計画
- □ **ideal** 名理想, 究極の目標 形理想的な, 申し分のない
- □ **identify** 動①(本人・同一と)確認する, 見分ける ②意気投合する
- □ **ignoring** 動ignore (無視する)の現在分詞
- □ **Iheya Island** 伊平屋島《沖縄本島の北西部にある県最北端の有人島》
- □ **Ikei Island** 伊計島《沖縄本島中部・勝連半島の北東に位置する》
- □ **Ikema** 名池間島《宮古島の北西に位置する》
- □ **immediate** 形さっそくの, 即座の, 直接の
- □ **impact** 名影響力, 反響, 効果
- □ **import** 動輸入する 名輸入, 輸入品
- □ **importance** 名重要性, 大切さ
- □ **important** 形重要な, 大切な, 有力な
- □ **Important Cultural Property** 重要文化財
- □ **improve** 動改善する[させる], 進歩する
- □ **in** 前①《場所・位置・所属》~(の中)に[で・の] ②《時》~(の時)に[の・で], ~後(に), ~の間(に) ③《方法・手段》~で ④~を身につけて, ~を着て ⑤~に関して, ~について ⑥《状態》~の状態で 副中へ[に], 内へ[に]
- □ **incense** 名香, 香料
- □ **incident** 名出来事, 事故, 事変 **Manchurian Incident**《the ‒ 》満州事変

- □ **include** 動含む, 勘定に入れる
- □ **including** 動include (含む)の現在分詞 前~を含めて, 込みで
- □ **income** 名収入, 所得, 収益
- □ **increase** 動増加[増強]する, 増やす, 増える 名増加(量), 増大
- □ **increasing** 動increase (増加する)の現在分詞 形増加する, 拡大する
- □ **incredible** 形①信じられない, 信用できない ②すばらしい, とてつもない
- □ **independent** 形独立した, 自立した
- □ **indigo** 名藍, 藍色
- □ **Indonesia** 名インドネシア《国名》
- □ **industry** 名産業, 工業
- □ **influence** 動影響をおよぼす
- □ **influential** 形影響力の大きい, 有力な
- □ **information** 名情報, 通知, 知識
- □ **injured** 動injure (痛める)の過去, 過去分詞 形負傷した, (名誉・感情などを)損ねられた
- □ **inland** 形①内陸の, 奥地の ②国内の, 内地の 副内陸に, 奥地に
- □ **inside** 名内部, 内側 形内部[内側]にある 副内部[内側]に 前~の内部[内側]に
- □ **instead** 副その代わりに **instead of**~の代わりに, ~をしないで
- □ **instrument** 名①道具, 器具, 器械 ②楽器
- □ **intangible** 形①触れられない, つかみどころのない ②(財産などが)無形の
- □ **intelligent** 形頭のよい, 聡明な
- □ **intensity** 名強烈さ, 激しさ
- □ **interesting** 動interest (興味を起こさせる)の現在分詞 形おもしろい, 興味を起こさせる
- □ **international** 形国際(間)の

□ **interpreter** 图解説者, 通訳

□ **intersection** 图交差点

□ **into** 前 ①《動作・運動の方向》〜の中へ[に] ②《変化》〜に[へ]

□ **invasion** 图侵略, 侵害

□ **invite** 動①招待する, 招く ②勧める, 誘う ③〜をもたらす

□ **involve** 動①含む, 伴う ②巻き込む, かかわらせる

□ **involved** 動 involve (含む) の過去, 過去分詞 形①巻き込まれている, 関連する ②入り組んだ, 込み入っている

□ **Irabu** 图伊良部島《沖縄県・宮古列島に属する島の一つ》

□ **Irabu Ohashi** 伊良部大橋《宮古島と伊良部島とを結ぶ橋》

□ **irabucha** 图イラブチャー《沖縄の方言で「ブダイ」のこと》

□ **Iriomote cat** イリオモテヤマネコ《西表島だけに生息するヤマネコ, 天然記念物》

□ **Iriomote Island** 西表島《沖縄県・八重山列島内で最大の面積を持つ》

□ **ironic** 形皮肉な, 反語的な

□ **is** 動 be (〜である) の3人称単数現在

□ **Ishigaki Island** 石垣島《沖縄県・八重山列島に属する島の一つ》

□ **Ishiganto** 图石敢當《文字が刻まれた魔除けの石碑や石標》

□ **island** 图島

□ **islander** 图島民

□ **issue** 图①問題, 論点 ②出口, 流出

□ **it** 代 ①それは[が], それを[に] ②《天候・日時・距離・寒暖などを示す》

□ **item** 图①項目, 品目 ②(新聞など) の記事

□ **Itoman** 图糸満《沖縄本島の最南端に位置する市》

□ **Itoman Haaree** 糸満ハーレー

《豊漁や海の安全を祈願する祭り》

□ **its** 代それの, あれの

□ **itself** 代それ自体, それ自身

□ **Izena Island** 伊是名島《沖縄本島の北西に位置する》

J

□ **January** 图1月

□ **Japan** 图日本《国名》

□ **Japanese** 形日本(人・語)の 图①日本人 ②日本語

□ **job** 图仕事, 職, 雇用

□ **join** 動①一緒になる, 参加する ②連結[結合]する, つなぐ 图結合

□ **journey** 图①(遠い目的地への) 旅 ②行程 動(長い) 旅行をする

□ **July** 图7月

□ **June** 图6月

□ **junior** 形年少の, 年下の 图年少者, 年下の者

□ **just** 形正しい, もっともな, 当然な 副①まさに, ちょうど, (〜した) ばかり ②ほんの, 単に, ただ〜だけ ③ちょっと

□ **Juuruku Nichi** ジュウルクニチ《沖縄で旧暦1月16日に行うお墓参り》

K

□ **Kachashi** 图カチャーシー《沖縄民謡に合わせて両手を挙げて左右に振り, 足を踏み鳴らす踊り》

□ **Kagoshima Prefecture** 鹿児島県

□ **kamaboko** 图かまぼこ

□ **Kanagawa Prefecture** 神奈川県

□ **Kanamaru** 图金丸《第一尚氏6代目王・尚泰久の重臣。後の第二尚氏初代国王・尚円。1415–1476》

□ **karate** 名空手

□ **kasuri** 名絣《染織模様の一種》

□ **Katsuren Castle** 勝連城《有力按司・阿麻和利（あまわり）の居城として有名。現在は城址となっている》

□ **keep** 動①とっておく，保つ，続ける ②（～を…に）しておく ③経営する ④守る **keep away** 近づけない

□ **kept** 動keep（とっておく）の過去，過去分詞

□ **Kerama Islands** 慶良間諸島《沖縄本島の西部に点在する島嶼群》

□ **kettle** 名なべ，やかん

□ **key** 名①かぎ，手がかり ②調子

□ **kill** 動殺す，消す，枯らす 名殺すこと

□ **kilometer** 名キロメートル《長さの単位》

□ **kimono** 名着物

□ **kindness** 名親切（な行為），優しさ

□ **king** 名王，国王

□ **kingdom** 名王国

□ **Kitadaito** 名北大東島《沖縄本島の東に位置する大東諸島の一つ》

□ **kitchen** 名台所，調理場

□ **know** 動①知っている，知る，（～が）わかる，理解している ②知り合いである

□ **known** 動know（知っている）の過去分詞 形知られた **known as**《be－》～として知られている

□ **koji** 名麹

□ **Konan High School** 興南高校《那覇市にある野球の強豪校》

□ **Korea** 名朝鮮，韓国《国名》

□ **kucha** 名クチャ《沖縄でしか取れない粘土質の土。貝やサンゴの死骸の堆積物》

□ **Kumejima** 名久米島《沖縄本島の西に位置する沖縄諸島の一つ》

□ **Kumiodori** 名組踊《琉球王国時代に成立した，沖縄の伝統的な音楽・舞踊・台詞で構成される歌舞劇》

□ **Kunigami** 名国頭《沖縄本島および周辺島嶼の北東地域》

□ **kunkunshi** 名工工四《三線の記譜法》

□ **Kurima** 名来間島《沖縄本島の南西に位置する宮古列島に属する》

□ **kusu** 名古酒（クース）《泡盛の中で3年以上熟成されたものを指す》

□ **Kyushu** 名九州

L

□ **lack** 動不足している，欠けている 名不足，欠乏

□ **lacquer** 名〔日本の〕漆

□ **laid** 動lay（置く）の過去，過去分詞

□ **lamp** 名ランプ，灯火

□ **land** 名①陸地，土地 ②国，領域 動上陸する，着地する

□ **landing** 動land（上陸する）の現在分詞 名上陸，着陸

□ **language** 名言語，言葉，国語，～語，専門語

□ **large** 形①大きい，広い ②大勢の，多量の **a large number of** 多くの～ 副①大きく ②自慢して

□ **last** 動続く，持ちこたえる

□ **later** 形もっと遅い，もっと後の 副後で，後ほど

□ **latitude** 名緯度

□ **law** 名法，法律

□ **lay out** ～の計画を立てる，段取りを決める

□ **layer** 名層，重ね 動層になる［する］

□ **lazy** 形怠惰な，無精な

□ **lead to** ～に至る，～に通じる，～を引き起こす

□ **leading** 動lead（導く）の現在分詞 形主要な，指導的な，先頭の

□ **learn** 動学ぶ, 習う, 教わる, 知識[経験]を得る

□ **least** 形いちばん小さい, 最も少ない 副いちばん小さく, 最も少なく 名最小, 最少 **at least** 少なくとも

□ **leave** 動①出発する, 去る ②残す, 置き忘れる ③(〜を…の)ままにしておく ④ゆだねる

□ **led** 動lead (導く) の過去, 過去分詞

□ **left** 名《the −》左, 左側 形左の, 左側の 副左に, 左側に 動leave (去る, 〜をあとに残す) の過去, 過去分詞

□ **leg** 名①脚, すね ②支柱

□ **legend** 名伝説, 伝説的人物, 言い伝え

□ **lend** 動貸す, 貸し出す

□ **less** 形〜より小さい[少ない] 副〜より少なく, 〜ほどでなく

□ **lesson** 名①授業, 学科, 課, けいこ ②教訓, 戒め

□ **let** 動(人に〜)させる, (〜するのを)許す, (〜をある状態に)する

□ **lettuce** 名レタス

□ **level** 名①水平, 平面 ②水準

□ **lie** 動①うそをつく ②横たわる, 寝る ③(ある状態に)ある, 存在する

□ **life** 名①生命, 生物 ②一生, 生涯, 人生 ③生活, 暮らし, 世の中 **way of life** 生き様, 生き方, 暮らし方

□ **lifestyle** 名生活様式, ライフスタイル

□ **like** 前〜に似ている, 〜のような **look like** 〜のように見える, 〜に似ている 形似ている, 〜のような 接あたかも〜のように

□ **likely** 形①ありそうな, (〜)しそうな ②適当な 副たぶん, おそらく

□ **line** 名①線, 糸, 電話線 ②(字の)行 ③列, (電車の)〜線

□ **linguist** 名言語学者

□ **link** 名①(鎖の)輪 ②リンク ③相互[因果]関係 動連結する, つながる

□ **lion** 名ライオン

□ **liqueur** 名リキュール, 混成酒《発酵酒や蒸留酒に果実などを浸して風味付けしたもの》

□ **list** 名名簿, 目録, 一覧表 動名簿[目録]に記入する

□ **liter** 名リットル, リッター

□ **little** 形①小さい, 幼い ②少しの, 短い ③ほとんど〜ない, 《a−》少しはある 名少し(しか), 少量 副全然〜ない, 《a−》少しはある

□ **live** 動住む, 暮らす, 生きている

□ **lively** 形①元気のよい, 活発な ②鮮やかな, 強烈な, 真に迫った

□ **lives** 名life (生命) の複数

□ **living** 動live (住む) の現在分詞 名生計, 生活 形①生きている, 現存の ②使用されている ③そっくりの

□ **local** 形地方の, ある場所[土地]の, 部分的な 名ある特定の地方のもの

□ **locally** 副①ある特定の場所[地方]で, 現地的に ②近くで, このあたり

□ **locate** 動置く, 居住する[させる]

□ **location** 名位置, 場所

□ **long** 形①長い, 長期の ②《長さ・距離・時間などを示す語句を伴って》〜の長さ[距離・時間]の 副長い間, ずっと 名長い期間 **before long** やがて, まもなく

□ **look** 動①見る ②(〜に)見える, (〜の)顔つきをする ③注意する ④《間投詞のように》ほら, ねえ **look like** 〜のように見える, 〜に似ている **look to** 〜しようとする 名①一見, 目つき ②外観, 外見, 様子

□ **loose** 形自由な, ゆるんだ, あいまいな 動ほどく, 解き放つ

□ **lord** 名首長, 主人, 領主

□ **lost** 動lose (失う) の過去, 過去分詞 形①失った, 負けた ②道に迷った, 困った

□ **lot** 名たくさん, たいへん, 《a − of

~ / -s of ~》たくさんの~

☐ **low** 形 ①低い, 弱い ②低級の, 劣等な 副 低く 名 低い水準[点]

☐ **low-cost airline** 《a ~》格安航空会社

☐ **lower** 形 もっと低い, 下級の, 劣った 動 下げる, 低くする

☐ **loyalty** 名 忠義, 忠誠

☐ **luck** 名 運, 幸運, めぐり合わせ

☐ **lunar** 形 月の, 月面の

☐ **luxury** 形 豪華な, 高級な, 贅沢な 名 豪華さ, 贅沢(品)

M

☐ **made** 動 make (作る) の過去, 過去分詞 be made from ~から作られる be made of ~でできて[作られて]いる be made to ~させられる be made up of ~で構成されている 形 作った, 作られた

☐ **magnificent** 形 壮大な, 壮麗な, すばらしい

☐ **main** 形 主な, 主要な

☐ **mainland** 名 本土, 大陸

☐ **maintain** 動 ①維持する ②養う

☐ **majimun** 名 マジムン《沖縄や奄美地方に伝わる魔物》

☐ **major** 形 大きいほうの, 主な, 一流の

☐ **make** 動 ①作る, 得る ②行う, (~に)なる ③(~を…に)する, (~を…)させる make a speech 演説をする make up 作り出す, 考え出す, ~を構成[形成]する make ~ into ~を…に仕立てる

☐ **making** 動 make (作る) の現在分詞 名 制作, 製造

☐ **male** 形 男の, 雄の 名 男, 雄

☐ **mammoth** 名 マンモス

☐ **man** 名 男性, 人, 人類

☐ **Manchurian Incident** 《the – 》満州事変

☐ **mango** 名 《果物》マンゴー

☐ **mangrove** 名 《植物》マングローブ, 紅樹林

☐ **manned** 形 〔宇宙船などが〕有人の

☐ **manufacture** 動 製造[製作]する 名 製造, 製作, 製品

☐ **many** 形 多数の, たくさんの so many 非常に多くの 代 多数(の人・物)

☐ **march** 名 ①行進 ②《M-》3月 動 行進する[させる], 進展する

☐ **Marine Corps** アメリカ海兵隊 **Marine Corps Air Station Futenma** 普天間飛行場

☐ **Marines** 名 海兵隊

☐ **marked** 動 mark (印をつける) の過去, 過去分詞 形 ①目立つ, 顕著な ②印のある, マークされた

☐ **martial** 形 ①戦争の, 戦争に適した ②軍人らしい, 勇ましい

☐ **mask** 名 面, マスク 動 マスクをつける

☐ **match** 名 試合, 勝負

☐ **May** 名 5月

☐ **meal** 名 ①食事 ②ひいた粉, あらびき粉

☐ **mean** 動 ①意味する ②(~のつもりで)言う, 意図する ③~するつもりである

☐ **meant** 動 mean (意味する) の過去, 過去分詞

☐ **medicine** 名 ①薬 ②医学, 内科

☐ **medieval** 形 中世の, 中世風の

☐ **meet** 動 ①会う, 知り合いになる ②合流する, 交わる ③(条件などに)達する, 合う

☐ **Meiji** 名 明治(時代)《1868–1912》

☐ **melon** 名 メロン

☐ **member** 名 一員, メンバー

105

□ **memorial** 名記念物, 記録 形記念の, 追悼の

□ **Memorial Day** 慰霊の日《6月23日。1945年のこの日、第二次世界大戦の沖縄戦が終結した》

□ **men** 名 man（男性）の複数

□ **mention** 動（〜について）述べる, 言及する 名言及, 陳述

□ **metal** 名金属, 合金

□ **method** 名①方法, 手段 ②秩序, 体系

□ **mibai** 名ミーバイ《沖縄の方言で「ハタ類の魚」のこと》

□ **mid** 形中央の, 中間の

□ **military** 形軍隊［軍人］の, 軍事の **military base** 軍事基地 名《the –》軍, 軍部

□ **millet** 名《植物》キビ, アワ

□ **million** 名①100万 ②《-s》数百万, 多数 形①100万の ②多数の

□ **mimiga** 名ミミガー《沖縄の方言で「豚の耳」のこと》

□ **mind** 名①心, 精神, 考え ②知性 動①気にする, いやがる ②気をつける, 用心する

□ **mineral** 名鉱物, 鉱石 形鉱物の

□ **mingle** 動入り混じる, 混ざる

□ **minsa** 名ミンサー織り《綿糸を使った沖縄の伝統的な織物技法》

□ **miserable** 形みじめな, 哀れな

□ **mistake** 名誤り, 誤解, 間違い 動間違える, 誤解する

□ **mix** 動①混ざる, 混ぜる ②（〜を）一緒にする 名混合（物）

□ **mixed** 動 mix（混ざる）の過去, 過去分詞 形混合の, 混ざった

□ **Miyako Island** 宮古島《沖縄本島の南西に位置する宮古列島の一つ》

□ **Miyakojima City Museum** 宮古島市総合博物館

□ **mold** 名かび

□ **momentous** 形重大な, 由々しき

□ **money** 名金, 通貨

□ **monorail** 名モノレール

□ **month** 名月, 1カ月

□ **monument** 名記念碑, 記念物

□ **moon** 名月, 月光

□ **moose** 名《動物》ヘラジカ, ムース

□ **more** 形①もっと多くの ②それ以上の, 余分の 副もっと, さらに多く, いっそう **more than** 〜以上 **no more than** ただの〜にすぎない **once more** もう一度 名もっと多くの物［人］

□ **most** 形①最も多い ②たいていの, 大部分の 代①大部分, ほとんど ②最多数, 最大限 副最も（多く）

□ **mostly** 副主として, 多くは, ほとんど

□ **mother** 名母, 母親

□ **mound** 名小山, 土手, 盛り土

□ **mount** 動（山などに）登る, （馬に）乗る, のせる 名山《ふつう Mt. と略して山名に用いる》

□ **Mount Omoto** 於茂登岳（おもとだけ）《沖縄県石垣市にある標高526ｍの山》

□ **mountain** 名①山 ②《the 〜 M-s》〜山脈 ③山のようなもの, 多量

□ **mouth** 名①口 ②言葉, 発言

□ **move** 動①動く, 動かす ②感動させる ③引っ越す, 移動する **move around** あちこち移動する **move to** 〜に引っ越す 名①動き, 運動 ②転居, 移動

□ **movement** 名①動き, 運動 ②《-s》行動 ③引っ越し ④変動

□ **moving** 動 move（動く）の現在分詞 形①動いている ②感動させる

□ **mozuku** 名モズク

□ **much** 形（量・程度が）多くの, 多量の 副①とても, たいへん ②《比較級・最上級を修飾して》ずっと, はるかに 名多量, たくさん, 重要なもの

- [ ] **mud** 名 ①泥, ぬかるみ ②つまら
ぬもの

- [ ] **muddy** 形 泥だらけの, ぬかるみの
動 泥まみれにする, 濁らせる

- [ ] **mugwort** 名 《植物》オオヨモギ,
オウシュウヨモギ

- [ ] **museum** 名 博物館, 美術館

- [ ] **music** 名 音楽, 楽曲

- [ ] **must** 助 ①～しなければならない
②～に違いない 名 絶対に必要なこ
と [もの]

N

- [ ] **Naha** 名 那覇市《沖縄県の県庁所在
地》

- [ ] **Naha Haarii** 那覇ハーリー《豊漁
や海の安全を祈願する祭り》

- [ ] **Nakabaru ruins** 仲原遺跡《沖縄
県・伊計島にある縄文後期～弥生前
期の村落跡》

- [ ] **Nakadomari (ruins)** 仲泊遺跡
《沖縄県恩納村にある沖縄先史時代の
遺跡》

- [ ] **Nakagusuku Castle** 中城城
《中城按司・護佐丸の居城跡》

- [ ] **Nakamura house** 中村家住宅
《18世紀中頃に建てられた歴史的建
造物, 重要文化財》

- [ ] **Nakijin Castle** 今帰仁城《琉球王
国成立以前に存在した北山王国の王
城跡》

- [ ] **name** 名 ①名前 ②名声 動 ①名前
をつける ②名指しする

- [ ] **Nansei Islands** 南西諸島《九州
南端から台湾北東にかけて位置する
島嶼群》

- [ ] **nation** 名 国, 国家《the –》国民

- [ ] **national** 形 国家 [国民] の, 全国の

- [ ] **natural** 形 ①自然の, 天然の ②生
まれつきの, 天性の ③当然な

- [ ] **naturally** 副 生まれつき, 自然に,

当然

- [ ] **nature** 名 自然 (界)

- [ ] **navigate** 動 航行する, 飛行する

- [ ] **near** 前 ～の近くに, ～のそばに 形
近い, 親しい 副 近くに, 親密で

- [ ] **nearby** 形 近くの, 間近の 副 近く
で, 間近で

- [ ] **nearly** 副 ①近くに, 親しく ②ほと
んど, あやうく

- [ ] **necklace** 名 ネックレス, 首飾り

- [ ] **need** 動 (～を) 必要とする, 必要で
ある 助 ～する必要がある

- [ ] **new** 形 ①新しい, 新規の ②新鮮な,
できたての

- [ ] **New Guinea** ニューギニア

- [ ] **New Year's Day** 元日

- [ ] **next** 形 ①次の, 翌～ ②隣の 副 ①
次に ②隣に 代 次の人 [もの]

- [ ] **nice** 形 すてきな, よい, きれいな,
親切な

- [ ] **nifaiyu** にーふぁいゆー《石垣島の
方言で「ありがとう」》

- [ ] **nife debiru** にふぇーでーびる《沖
縄本島の方言で「ありがとう」》

- [ ] **nigana** 名 ニガナ《沖縄の方言で「ホ
ソバワダン (キク科の多年草) 」を指
す》

- [ ] **nigari** 名 ニガリ《海水から塩を抽出
する際にできる液体。豆腐づくりの凝
固剤として使われる》

- [ ] **night** 名 夜, 晩

- [ ] **nine** 名 9 (の数字), 9人 [個] 形 9の,
9人 [個] の

- [ ] **Nirai Kanai** ニライカナイ《沖縄
や奄美地方に伝わる, 海の彼方や海底
にあるとされる理想郷の伝承》

- [ ] **no** 副 ①いいえ, いや ②少しも～な
い no more than ただの～にすぎな
い 形 ～がない, 少しも～ない, ～ど
ころでない, ～禁止 名 否定, 拒否

- [ ] **noise** 名 騒音, 騒ぎ, 物音

- [ ] **normal** 形 普通の, 平均の, 標準的

な 图平常, 標準, 典型

- □ **normally** 副普通は, 通常は

- □ **north** 图《the – 》北, 北部 形北の, 北からの 副北へ [に], 北から

- □ **northern** 形北の, 北向きの, 北からの

- □ **not** 副~でない, ~しない not only ~ but (also) … ~だけでなく…もまた

- □ **nothing** 代何も~ない [しない]

- □ **November** 图11月

- □ **now** 副①今 (では), 現在 ②今すぐに ③では, さて 图今, 現在 形今の, 現在の

- □ **Nuchidu Takara** 命どぅ宝《「命こそ宝＝生きていることにこそ意味がある」という沖縄の人々が大切にする思想》

- □ **number** 图①数, 数字, 番号 ②~号, ~番 ③《-s》多数 a large number of 多くの~ 動番号をつける, 数える

- □ **nutrient** 图栄養物, 栄養になる食物, 栄養素

- □ **nutritional** 形栄養の [に関する]

O

- □ **obey** 動服従する, (命令などに) 従う

- □ **object** 图①物, 事物 ②目的物, 対象 動反対する, 異議を唱える

- □ **Obon** 图お盆《日本で夏季に行われる祖先の霊を祀る一連の行事》

- □ **occasion** 图①場合, (特定の) 時 ②機会, 好機 ③理由, 根拠

- □ **ocean** 图海, 大洋《the ~ O-》~洋

- □ **oceanic** 形大洋の, 大洋に関する

- □ **October** 图10月

- □ **of** 前①《所有・所属・部分》~の, ~に属する ②《性質・特徴・材料》~の, ~製の ③《部分》~のうち ④《分離・除去》~から

- □ **off** 副①離れて ②はずれて ③止まって ④休んで give off 発散する, 放つ 形①離れて ②季節はずれの ③休みの 前①~を離れて, ~をはずれて, (値段が) ~引きの

- □ **offer** 動申し出る, 申し込む, 提供する 图提案, 提供

- □ **officer** 图役人, 警察官, 将校, 司令官

- □ **official** 形①公式の, 正式の ②職務上の, 公の

- □ **often** 副しばしば, たびたび

- □ **oink** 图ブタの鳴き声, ブーブー

- □ **Okinawa** 图沖縄(県, 市, 本島, 諸島)《地名》

- □ **Okinawa Island** 沖縄本島 图《the – 》軍, 軍部

- □ **Okinawa Prefectural Peace Memorial Museum** 沖縄県平和祈念資料館

- □ **Okinawan** 图沖縄人, 沖縄県民 形沖縄人の, 沖縄県民の

- □ **Okinawa rail** ヤンバルクイナ《沖縄本島北部の固有種》

- □ **Okinawa woodpecker** ノグチゲラ《沖縄本島北部の固有種》

- □ **old** 形①年取った, 老いた ②~歳の ③古い, 昔の 图昔, 老人

- □ **Olympic** 形①オリンピックの ②《the O- games》オリンピック大会

- □ **on** 前①《場所・接触》~ (の上) に ②《日・時》~に, ~と同時に, ~のすぐ後で ③《関係・従事》~に関して, ~について, ~して 副①身につけて, 上に ②前へ, 続けて

- □ **once** 副①一度, 1回 ②かつて once more もう一度 图一度, 1回 接いったん~すると

- □ **one** 图1 (の数字), 1人 [個] one of ~の1つ [人] 形①1の, 1人 [個] の ②ある~ ③《the – 》唯一の 代①(一般の) 人, ある物 ②一方, 片方 ③~

なもの

□ **only** 形唯一の 副①単に、〜にすぎない、ただ〜だけ ②やっと not only 〜 but (also) … 〜だけでなく …もまた 接ただし、だがしかし

□ **Onna Village** 恩納村《沖縄本島の中央部に位置する島》

□ **open** 形①開いた、広々とした 公開された 動①開く、始まる ②広がる、広げる ③打ち明ける

□ **opinion** 名意見、見識、世論、評判

□ **option** 名選択(の余地)、選択可能物、選択権

□ **or** 接①〜か…、または ②さもないと ③すなわち、言い換えると

□ **ordinary** 形①普通の、通常の ②並の、平凡な

□ **ornamental** 形装飾の、飾りの

□ **other** 形①ほかの、異なった ②(2つのうち)もう一方の、(3つ以上のうち)残りの 代①ほかの人[物] ②《the –》残りの1つ each other お互いに 副そうでなく、別に

□ **otori** 名オトーリ《宮古列島に伝わる飲酒の風習。車座になって泡盛を飲む酒宴の席で行われる》

□ **out** 副①外へ[に]、不在で、離れて ②世に出て ③消えて ④すっかり lay out 〜の計画を立てる、段取りを決める work out 考え出す、答えが出る、〜の結果になる 形①外の、遠く離れた ②公表された 前〜から外へ[に]

□ **outside** 名外部、外側 形外部の、外側の 副外へ、外側に 前〜の外に[で・の・へ]、〜の範囲を越えて

□ **over** 前①〜の上の[に]、〜を一面に覆って ②〜を越えて、〜以上に、〜よりまさって ③〜の向こう側の[に] ④〜の間 all over 〜中で、〜の至る所で over time 時間とともに、そのうち 副上に、一面に、ずっと rule over 治める、統御する take over 引き継ぐ、支配する、乗っ取る watch over 見守る、見張る 形①上部の、上

位の、過多の ②終わって、すんで

□ **overseas** 形海外の、外国の 副海外へ 名国外

□ **overview** 名概観、大要、あらまし

□ **own** 形自身の 動持っている、所有する

□ **owner** 名持ち主、オーナー

□ **oya** 名親《「オトーリ」で口上を述べて酒を飲み干す役》

P

□ **Paantu** 名パーントゥ《宮古島の伝統的な厄払い行事。仮面をつけた神「パーントゥ」が集落を回って地域の厄を払い、福を呼ぶ》

□ **paarankuu** 名パーランクー《エイサー等で使われる方張りの小太鼓》

□ **pacific** 形《the P-》太平洋

□ **Pacific Ocean** 太平洋

□ **Pacific War** 太平洋戦争

□ **pack** 動〜を詰め込む、パックする、包装する

□ **pair** 名(2つから成る)一対、一組、ペア 動対になる[する]

□ **palm** 名手のひら(状のもの)

□ **papaya** 名《植物》パパイヤ(の実)

□ **paradise** 名①天国 ②地上の楽園

□ **parasailing** 名パラセーリング《パラシュートを装着し、モーターボートなどで引いてもらい空中浮遊を楽しむスポーツ》

□ **parent** 名《-s》両親

□ **park** 名①公園、広場 ②駐車場 動駐車する

□ **part** 名①部分、割合 ②役目 動分ける、分かれる、別れる

□ **particularly** 副特に、とりわけ

□ **partly** 副一部分は、ある程度は

□ **party** 名パーティー、会、集まり

□ **pass** 動①過ぎる, 通る ②(年月が)たつ ③手渡す **pass by** ～のそばを通る[通り過ぎる] **pass down**(次の世代に)伝える **pass on** ①通り過ぎる ②(情報などを他者に)伝える **pass through** ～を通る, 通行する

□ **passing** 動 pass(過ぎる)の現在分詞

□ **past** 形過去の, この前の 名過去(の出来事)

□ **path** 名①(踏まれてできた)小道, 歩道 ②進路, 通路

□ **pay** 動①支払う, 払う, 報いる, 償う ②割に合う, ペイする 名給料, 報い

□ **payment** 名支払い, 払い込み

□ **peace** 名①平和, 和解,《the－》治安 ②平穏, 静けさ

□ **peaceful** 形平和な, 穏やかな

□ **peak** 名頂点, 最高点 動最高になる, ピークに達する

□ **people** 名①(一般に)人々 ②民衆, 世界の人々, 国民, 民族 ③人間

□ **per** 前～につき, ～ごとに

□ **percent** 名パーセント, 百分率

□ **perfect** 形①完璧な, 完全な ②純然たる 動完成する, 改良[改善]する

□ **perform** 動①(任務などを)行う, 果たす, 実行する ②演じる, 演奏する

□ **period** 名①期, 期間, 時代 ②ピリオド, 終わり **Gusuku period**《the－》グスク時代 **Prehistoric period**《the－》先史時代 動《－on～》～に基礎を置く, 基づく

□ **Perry** 名《Commodore－》ペリー提督《マシュー・カルブレイス・ペリー（Matthew Calbraith Perry）アメリカ海軍の軍人, 1794–1858》

□ **person** 名①人 ②人格, 人柄

□ **personal** 形①個人の, 私的な ②本人自らの

□ **personnel** 名人材, 人員, 人事課 形職員の, 人事の

□ **Peru** 名ペルー《国名》

□ **Philippines** 名フィリピン《国名》

□ **pig** 名ブタ(豚)

□ **pigment** 名〔水や油で溶く〕顔料

□ **pile** 動積み重なる, 堆積する **pile up** 積み重ねる

□ **pineapple** 名パイナップル

□ **pit** 名(地面の)穴, くぼみ, ピット, わきの下 動穴を作る, 掘る, へこませる

□ **place** 名①場所, 建物 ②余地, 空間 ③《one's－》家, 部屋 **in place of**～の代わりに **take place** 行われる, 起こる **take the place of**～の代わりをする 動①置く, 配置する ②任命する, 任じる

□ **plan** 名計画, 設計(図), 案 動計画する **plan to do**～するつもりである

□ **plane** 名①飛行機 ②平面, 面 形平らな, 平面の

□ **plant** 名①植物, 草木 ②設備, プラント, 工場 動植えつける, すえつける

□ **plaque** 名①額, 飾り板 ②歯垢

□ **plaster** 名しっくい, 壁土, 石膏

□ **plate** 名①(浅い)皿, 1皿の料理 ②金属板, 標札, プレート

□ **play** 動①遊ぶ, 競技する ②(楽器を)演奏する, (役を)演じる 名遊び, 競技, 劇

□ **plenty** 名十分, たくさん, 豊富 **plenty of** たくさんの～

□ **point** 名①先, 先端 ②点 ③地点, 時点, 箇所 ④《the－》要点 動①(～を)指す, 向ける ②とがらせる

□ **poison** 名①毒, 毒薬 ②害になるもの 動毒を盛る, 毒する

□ **policy** 名政策, 方針, 手段

□ **political** 形①政治の, 政党の ②策略的な

110

□ **poor** 形 ①貧しい, 乏しい, 粗末な, 貧弱な ②劣った, へたな ③不幸な, 哀れな, 気の毒な

□ **popular** 形 ①人気のある, 流行の ②一般的な, 一般向きの

□ **popularity** 名 人気, 流行

□ **population** 名 人口, 住民(数)

□ **pork** 名 豚肉

□ **position** 名 ①位置, 場所, 姿勢 ②地位, 身分, 職 ③立場, 状況 動 置く, 配置する

□ **possibility** 名 可能性, 見込み, 将来性

□ **possible** 形 ①可能な ②ありうる, 起こりうる

□ **post** 名 持ち場, 部署, 地位

□ **pot** 名 壺, (深い)なべ 動 壺に入れる, 鉢植えにする

□ **pottery** 名 陶器

□ **power** 名 力, 能力, 才能, 勢力, 権力 power struggle 権力闘争, 勢力争い

□ **practice** 名 ①実行, 実践 ②練習 ③慣習 ④やり方, 方法 動 実行する, 練習[訓練]する

□ **pray** 動 祈る, 懇願する pray for ~のために祈る

□ **prayer** 名 ①祈り, 祈願(文) ②祈る人

□ **precious** 形 ①貴重な, 高価な ②かわいい, 大事な

□ **predict** 動 予測[予想]する

□ **preface** 名 序文, 序論

□ **prefectural** 形 県の, 県立の

□ **prefecture** 名 県, 府

□ **Prehistoric period** 《the – 》先史時代

□ **prepare** 動 ①準備[用意]をする ②覚悟する[させる]

□ **preserve** 動 保存[保護]する, 保つ

□ **price** 名 ①値段, 代価 ②《-s》物価,

相場 動 値段をつける, 値段を聞く

□ **priestess** 名 巫女, 女性の祭司

□ **private** 形 ①私的な, 個人の ②民間の, 私立の

□ **problem** 名 問題, 難問

□ **product** 名 ①製品, 産物 ②成果, 結果

□ **production** 名 製造, 生産

□ **professional** 形 専門の, プロの, 職業的な 名 専門家, プロ

□ **profit** 名 利益, 利潤, ため 動 利益になる, (人の)ためになる, 役立つ

□ **profitable** 形 利益になる, 有益な

□ **project** 名 ①計画, プロジェクト ②研究課題

□ **promote** 動 促進する, 昇進[昇級]させる

□ **proper** 形 ①適した, 適切な, 正しい ②固有の

□ **property** 名 財産, 所有物[地]

□ **prosperity** 名 繁栄, 繁盛, 成功

□ **protect** 動 保護する, 防ぐ

□ **protection** 名 保護, 保護するもの[人]

□ **protein** 名 タンパク質, プロテイン

□ **provide** 動 ①供給する, 用意する, (~に)備える ②規定する

□ **public** 名 一般の人々, 大衆 形 公の, 公開の

□ **publish** 動 ①発表[公表]する ②出版[発行]する

□ **punish** 動 罰する, ひどい目にあわせる

□ **put** 動 ①置く, のせる ②入れる, つける ③(ある状態に)する ④put の過去, 過去分詞 put an end to ~に終止符を打つ, ~を終わらせる, ~に決着をつける put in ~の中に入れる

Q

□ **quickly** 副敏速に, 急いで

R

□ **race** 名①競争, 競走 ②人種, 種族 動①競争［競走］する ②疾走する

□ **racing** 名競走, 競艇

□ **rafute** 名ラフテー《沖縄の郷土料理で「豚の角煮」のこと》

□ **Raiho-shin** 来訪神《年に一度, 決まった時期に人間の世界に来訪するとされる神》

□ **rail** 名①横木, 手すり ②レール, 鉄道

□ **rain** 名雨, 降雨 動①雨が降る ②雨のように降る［降らせる］

□ **raise** 動①上げる, 高める ②起こす ③〜を育てる ④(資金を)調達する

□ **ramie** 名カラムシ《イラクサ科の多年生植物。茎の表皮から作った糸が宮古上布の材料となる》

□ **ran** 動 run (走る)の過去

□ **range** 名列, 連なり, 範囲 動①並ぶ, 並べる ②およぶ

□ **rapidly** 副速く, 急速, すばやく, 迅速に

□ **rare** 形①まれな, 珍しい, 逸品の ②希薄な

□ **rat** 名①ネズミ(鼠) ②裏切り者

□ **rate** 名①割合, 率 ②相場, 料金 動①見積もる, 評価する［される］ ②等級をつける

□ **rather** 副①むしろ, かえって ②かなり, いくぶん, やや ③それどころか逆に

□ **reach** 動①着く, 到着する, 届く ②手を伸ばして取る 名手を伸ばすこと, (手の)届く範囲

□ **read** 動読む, 読書する

□ **real** 形実際の, 実在する, 本物の 副本当に

□ **really** 副本当に, 実際に, 確かに

□ **realm** 名王国, 領土

□ **reason** 名①理由 ②理性, 道理 動①推論する ②説き伏せる

□ **rebuild** 動再建する, 改造する

□ **rebuilt** 動 rebuild (再建する)の過去, 過去分詞

□ **receive** 動①受け取る, 受領する ②迎える, 迎え入れる

□ **recent** 形近ごろの, 近代の

□ **recently** 副近ごろ, 最近

□ **recover** 動①取り戻す, ばん回する ②回復する

□ **recycle** 動再生利用する, 再循環させる

□ **red** 形赤い red soil 赤土 名赤, 赤色

□ **reddish-brown** 赤味を帯びた茶色(の)

□ **reduce** 動①減じる ②しいて〜させる, (〜の)状態にする

□ **reef** 名暗礁, 岩礁

□ **refill** 動詰め替える, 補充する

□ **reflect** 動映る, 反響する, 反射する

□ **regarding** 前〜に関しては, 〜について

□ **region** 名①地方, 地域 ②範囲

□ **register** 動登録する

□ **registered** 動 register (登録する)の過去, 過去分詞 形登録された

□ **registration** 名登録, 記載, 登記

□ **regular** 形①規則的な, 秩序のある ②定期的な, 一定の, 習慣的な

□ **reinforce** 動補強［強化］する, 拍車をかける

□ **rejoin** 動復帰する, 再び一緒になる

□ **related** 動 relate (関係がある)の過去, 過去分詞 形①関係のある, 関連した ②姻戚の

- **relationship** 名関係, 関連, 血縁関係
- **religion** 名宗教, ～教, 信条
- **rely** 動（人が…に）頼る, 当てにする
- **remain** 動①残っている, 残る ②（～の）ままである［いる］ 名《-s》①残り（もの） ②遺跡
- **remember** 動思い出す, 覚えている, 忘れないでいる
- **remote** 形①（距離・時間的に）遠い, 遠隔の ②人里離れた
- **rent** 動賃借りする 名使用料, 賃貸料
- **repeat** 動繰り返す 名繰り返し, 反復, 再演
- **repeated** 動repeat（繰り返す）の過去, 過去分詞 形繰り返された, 度重なる
- **replace** 動①取り替える, 差し替える ②元に戻す
- **report** 動①報告［通知・発表］する ②記録する, 記事を書く 名①報告, レポート ②（新聞の）記事, 報道
- **represent** 動①表現する ②意味する ③代表する
- **require** 動①必要とする, 要する ②命じる, 請求する
- **resident** 名居住者, 在住者
- **resort** 名①行楽地, リゾート ②頼みの綱, 頼り 動①手段に訴える ②行く, 通う
- **resource** 名①資源, 財産 ②手段, 方策
- **rest** 名①休息 ②安静 ③休止, 停止 ④《the –》残り
- **restaurant** 名レストラン, 料理店, 食堂
- **result** 名結果, 成り行き, 成績 **as a result** その結果（として）
- **return** 動帰る, 戻る, 返す **return to** ～に戻る, ～に帰る 名①帰還, 返却 ②返答, 報告（書）, 申告

- **rhythm** 名リズム, 調子
- **rib** 名肋骨, 肋骨状のもの, あばら肉
- **rice** 名米, 飯
- **rice cake** 餅
- **rich** 形①富んだ, 金持ちの ②豊かな, 濃い, 深い 名裕福な人
- **ride** 動乗る, 乗って行く, 馬に乗る 名乗ること
- **right** 名《the –》右, ライト
- **ring** 動①輪で取り囲む ②鳴る, 鳴らす ③電話をかける
- **rise** 動①昇る, 上がる ②生じる 名①上昇, 上がること ②発生
- **rising** 形昇る, 高まる
- **rivalry** 名競争, ライバル, 敵対
- **river** 名①川 ②（溶岩などの）大量流出
- **road** 名①道路, 道, 通り ②手段, 方法
- **rock** 名①岩, 岸壁, 岩石 ②揺れること, 動揺 動揺れる, 揺らす
- **roof** 名屋根（のようなもの）, 住居 動屋根をつける
- **root** 名①根, 根元 ②根源, 原因 ③《-s》先祖, ルーツ
- **rose** 動rise（昇る）の過去
- **round** 副①回って ②周りに 名①円, 球, 輪 ②回転 前①～を回って ②～の周囲に
- **royal** 形王の, 女王の, 国立の
- **ruin** 名破滅, 減亡, 破産, 廃墟 動破減させる
- **rule** 名①規則, ルール ②支配 動支配する **rule over** 治める, 統御する
- **ruler** 名①支配者 ②定規
- **run** 動走る
- **Ryukyu** 名琉球《地域名, 琉球諸島は奄美群島・沖縄諸島・宮古列島・八重山列島の総体》
- **Ryukyu Kingdom** 琉球王国

113

《1429年から1879年までの間, 琉球諸島を中心に存在した王国》

☐ **Ryukyu limestone** 琉球石灰岩

☐ **Ryukyu spiny rat** アマミトゲネズミ《奄美大島の固有種》

☐ **Ryukyuan** 图琉球人 形琉球人の

☐ **Ryukyuan Dance** 琉球舞踊《琉球, 沖縄県内で継承されている舞踊の総称》

S

☐ **sabani** 图サバニ《南西諸島の伝統的な漁船。糸満ハーレーに用いられる》

☐ **sacred** 形神聖な, 厳粛な

☐ **sadly** 副悲しそうに, 不幸にも

☐ **safety** 图安全, 無事, 確実

☐ **said** 動say (言う) の過去, 過去分詞

☐ **sail** 動帆走する, 航海する, 出航する

☐ **sailor** 图船員, (ヨットの) 乗組員

☐ **sake** 图 (〜の) ため, 利益, 目的

☐ **salt** 图塩, 食塩

☐ **saltiness** 图塩味

☐ **salty** 形塩の, 塩を含む

☐ **same** 形①同じ, 同様の ②前述のthe same 〜 as [that] ……と同じ (ような) 〜 代《the –》同一の人 [物] 副《the –》同様に

☐ **samurai** 图侍

☐ **sand** 图①砂 ②《-s》砂漠, 砂浜

☐ **sandy** 形砂の, 砂だらけの, 砂のような

☐ **sank** 動sink (沈む) の過去

☐ **sanshin** 图三線《琉球王国で独自に発展した弦楽器の一種》

☐ **Sanzan** 图三山 (時代)《沖縄本島で北山・中山・南山の三王国が割拠していた時代。1322頃–1429》

☐ **sash** 图サッシュ《腰に付ける幅広の帯》

☐ **Satsuma (Domain)** 薩摩藩

☐ **save** 動①救う, 守る ②とっておく, 節約する

☐ **saw** 動see (見る) の過去

☐ **say** 動言う, 口に出す 图言うこと, 言い分

☐ **saying** 動say (言う) の現在分詞 图ことわざ, 格言, 発言

☐ **scale** 图①目盛り ②規模, 割合, 程度, スケール ③《音楽》音階

☐ **scholar** 图学者

☐ **school** 图学校, 校舎, 授業 (時間)

☐ **schoolchildren** 图schoolchild (学童) の複数

☐ **scolding** 動scold (叱る) の現在分詞 图叱ること, 小言

☐ **sea** 图海.《the 〜 S, the S- of 〜》〜海

☐ **seafood** 图海産物

☐ **seawater** 图海水

☐ **seaweed** 图海藻, 海草

☐ **second** 图①第2 (の人 [物]) ②(時間の) 秒, 瞬時 形第2の, 2番の

☐ **Second Sho Dynasty** 《the –》第二尚氏王統《1469–1879》

☐ **Second Sino-Japanese War** 《the –》日中戦争

☐ **secretly** 副秘密に, 内緒で

☐ **section** 图①断片 ②区分, 区域 ③部門, 課

☐ **sector** 图①(産業などの) 部門, セクター ②(幾何で) 扇形

☐ **security** 图安全 (性), 安心 **US-Japan Security Treaty**《the –》日米安全保障条約

☐ **see** 動①見る, 見える, 見物する ②(〜と) わかる, 認識する, 経験する ③会う ④考える, 確かめる, 調べる ⑤気をつける

☐ **seen** 動see (見る) の過去分詞 be

seen as ～として見られる

□ **Sefa Utaki** 斎場御嶽（せーふぁぅたき）《沖縄県南城市にある史跡。「御嶽」は琉球の信仰における聖域のこと》

□ **self-defense** 图自衛, 自己防衛, 正当防衛

□ **sell** 動売る, 売っている, 売れる

□ **send** 動①送る, 届ける ②（人を～に）行かせる

□ **senior** 厖年長の, 年上の, 古参の, 上級の 图年長者, 先輩, 先任者

□ **sent** 動 send（送る）の過去, 過去分詞

□ **serve** 動①仕える, 奉仕する ②（客の）応対をする, 給仕する, 食事［飲み物］を出す ③（役目を）果たす, 務める, 役に立つ

□ **service** 图①勤務, 業務 ②公益事業 ③奉仕, 貢献

□ **set** 動①置く, 当てる, つける ②整える, 設定する ③（～を…の状態に）する, させる ④setの過去, 過去分詞 **set up** 設置する, 定める 图一そろい, セット

□ **settle** 動～に移り住む, 定住する

□ **seventeenth** 图17, 17人［個］ 厖17の, 17人［個］の

□ **severely** 副厳しく, 簡素に

□ **shape** 動①形, 姿, 型 ②状態, 調子 動形づくる, 具体化する

□ **share** 動分配する, 共有する

□ **shell** 图①貝がら, （木の実・卵などの）から ②（建物の）骨組み **Age of Shells《the－》**貝の時代

□ **shield** 图盾, 防御物 動保護する, 遮蔽する

□ **shift** 動移す, 変える, 転嫁する 图①変化, 移動 ②交替, （交代制の）勤務（時間）, シフト

□ **Shiimii** シーミー《沖縄の方言で「清明祭」を指す。旧暦3月初旬に親類が揃って墓参し, 墓前で祖先と共にごちそうを食べる行事》

□ **Shikina-en** 图識名園《那覇市にある史跡。琉球王家最大の別邸で, 国王一家の保養や外国使臣の接待などに利用された》

□ **shima dofu** 島豆腐《沖縄県の豆腐。沖縄豆腐とも呼ばれる》

□ **shima yasai** 島野菜《沖縄県の伝統野菜》

□ **Shimazu clan** 島津氏

□ **Shimoji Island** 下地島《沖縄本島の南西に位置する宮古列島の島の一つ》

□ **shine** 動①光る, 輝く ②光らせる, 磨く 图光, 輝き

□ **Shinto** 图神道

□ **ship** 图船, 飛行船 動①船に積む, 運送する ②乗船する

□ **shipping** 图配送, 船積み, 海運業, 船舶輸送

□ **shisa** 图シーサー《沖縄に伝わる獅子像。魔除けとして家屋の屋根や門に取り付ける》

□ **Sho En** 尚円《琉球王国・第二尚氏王統の初代国王。1415-1476》

□ **Sho Hashi** 尚巴志《琉球王国・第一尚氏王統。第2代目の中山王。1372-1439》

□ **Sho Nei** 尚寧《琉球王国・第二尚氏王統。第7代目の国王。1564-1620》

□ **Sho Tai** 尚泰《琉球王国・第二尚氏王統。第19代目（最後）の国王。1843-1901》

□ **Sho Taikyu** 尚泰久《琉球王国・第一尚氏王統。第6代目の国王。1415-1460》

□ **Sho Toku** 尚徳《琉球王国・第一尚氏王統。第7代目（最後）の国王。1441-1469》

□ **shogunate** 图将軍の職［政治］

□ **show** 動①見せる, 示す, 見える ②明らかにする, 教える 图案内する

□ **shrine** 图廟, 聖堂, 神社

□ **Shuri Castle** 首里城《那覇市にあ

る城跡。歴代琉球国王の居城として有名》

- **side** 名 側, 横, そば, 斜面

- **Siberia** 名 シベリア

- **Siberian** 名 シベリア人 形 シベリアの, シベリア人の

- **sight** 名 ①見ること, 視力, 視界 ②光景, 眺め ③見解

- **sign** 名 ①きざし, 徴候 ②跡 ③記号 ④身振り, 合図, 看板

- **silence** 名 沈黙, 無言, 静寂

- **silk** 名 絹(布), 生糸 形 絹の, 絹製の

- **similar** 形 同じような, 類似した, 相似の

- **simple** 形 ①単純な, 簡単な, 質素な ②単一の, 単独の ③普通の, ただの

- **simply** 副 ①簡単に ②単に, ただ ③まったく, 完全に

- **since** 接 ①～以来 ②～だから 前 ～以来 副 それ以来

- **single-handedly** 副 人の手を借りずに, 独力で, 自力で

- **sink** 動 沈む, 沈める, 落ち込む 名 (台所の)流し

- **Sino-Japanese** 形 中国–日本間の

- **sit** 動 ①座る, 腰掛ける ②止まる ③位置する

- **site** 名 位置, 敷地, 用地 動 (ある場所に建物を)設ける, 位置させる

- **situation** 名 ①場所, 位置 ②状況, 境遇, 立場

- **sixth** 形 第6番目(の人・物), 6日 形 第6番目の

- **size** 名 大きさ, 寸法, サイズ 動 (大きさに従って)分類する, 測る

- **slight** 形 ①わずかな ②ほっそりして ②とるに足らない

- **slightly** 副 わずかに, いささか

- **slowly** 副 遅く, ゆっくり

- **small** 形 ①小さい, 少ない ②取るに足りない 副 小さく, 細かく

- **smooth** 形 滑らかな, すべすべした 動 滑らかにする, 平らにする

- **snakeskin** 名 ヘビ革

- **snorkeling** 名 シュノーケリング

- **so** 副 ①とても ②同様に, ～もまた ③《先行する句・節の代用》そのように, そう so many 非常に多くの so that ～するために, それで, ～できるように 接 ①だから, それで ②では, さて and so そこで, それだから

- **soccer** 名 サッカー

- **soft** 形 柔らかい, 手ざわり[口あたり]のよい

- **soil** 名 土, 土地 red soil 赤土

- **sold** 動 sell(売る)の過去, 過去分詞

- **soldier** 名 兵士, 兵卒

- **solve** 動 解く, 解決する

- **some** 形 ①いくつかの, 多少の ②ある, 誰か, 何か 副 約, およそ 代 ①いくつか ②ある人[物]たち

- **someone** 代 ある人, 誰か take someone in 身柄を引き取る

- **song** 名 歌, 詩歌, 鳴き声

- **Sonohyan Utaki** 園比屋武御嶽(そのひゃんうたき)《沖縄県那覇市にある史跡。「御嶽」は琉球の信仰における聖域のこと》

- **sotetsu-jigoku** ソテツ地獄《大正から昭和初期にかけて南西諸島において発生した経済恐慌》

- **sound** 名 音, 騒音, 響き, サウンド

- **source** 名 源, 原因, もと

- **south** 名 《the –》南, 南方, 南部 形 南の, 南方[南部]の

- **South America** 南アメリカ(大陸)

- **southeast** 名 南東(部) 形 南東の, 南東向きの

- **Southeast Asia** 東南アジア

□ **Southeast Asian** 東南アジア人

□ **southern** 形南の, 南向きの, 南からの

□ **southward** 副南方へ

□ **southwest** 名南西(部) 形南西の, 南西向きの 副南西へ, 南西から

□ **souvenir** 名おみやげ

□ **soybean** 名大豆

□ **space** 名①空間, 宇宙 ②すき間, 余地, 場所, 間

□ **speak** 動話す, 言う, 演説する

□ **speaking** 動 speak (話す) の現在分詞 名話すこと, 談話, 演説

□ **special** 形①特別の, 特殊の, 臨時の ②専門の

□ **specialty** 名特産品, 名産

□ **spectacular** 形壮観な

□ **speech** 名演説, 言語, 語 **make a speech** 演説をする

□ **spice** 名スパイス, 香辛料

□ **spiny** 形とげの(ある), とげで覆われた

□ **spirit** 名①霊 ②精神, 気力

□ **spoke** 動 speak (話す) の過去

□ **spoken** 動 speak (話す) の過去分詞 形口語の

□ **sport** 名①スポーツ ②《-s》競技会, 運動会

□ **sport-loving** スポーツ好きの

□ **spot** 名地点, 場所, 立場

□ **spread** 動①広がる, 広げる, 伸びる, 伸ばす ②塗る, まく, 散布する 名広がり, 拡大

□ **spring** 名①春 ②泉, 源 ③ばね, ぜんまい 動跳ねる, 跳ぶ

□ **stable** 形安定した, 堅固な, 分解しにくい 名馬小屋, 厩舎

□ **standard** 名標準, 規格, 規準 形①標準の ②一流の, 優秀な

□ **start** 動①出発する, 始まる, 始める ②生じる, 生じさせる **start**
doing ～し始める 名出発, 開始

□ **state** 名①あり様, 状態 ②国家, (アメリカなどの) 州 ③階層, 地位 動述べる, 表明する

□ **station** 名《軍事》駐屯地 **air station** 航空基地

□ **statue** 名像

□ **stay** 動①とどまる, 泊まる, 滞在する ②持続する, (～の)ままでいる **stay in** (場所) に泊まる, 滞在する 名滞在

□ **steadily** 副しっかりと

□ **steel** 名鋼, 鋼鉄(製の物) 形鋼鉄の, 堅い

□ **step** 名①歩み, 1歩(の距離) ②段階 ③踏み段, 階段 動歩む, 踏む

□ **stewed** 形《料理》とろ火で煮込んだ

□ **still** 副①まだ, 今でも ②それでも(なお) 形静止した, 静かな

□ **stone** 名①石, 小石 ②宝石 形石の, 石製の

□ **stop** 動①やめる, やめさせる, 止める, 止まる ②立ち止まる 名①停止 ②停留所, 駅

□ **straight** 形①一線の, まっすぐな, 直立[垂直]の ②率直な, 整然とした 副①一直線に, まっすぐに, 垂直に ②率直に 名一直線, ストレート

□ **strange-looking** 形外観[外見]が奇妙な, 見た目の変な

□ **strategic** 形戦略的な, 戦略上の

□ **street** 名①街路 ②《S-》～通り

□ **strengthen** 動強くする, しっかりさせる

□ **stretch** 動引き伸ばす, 広がる, 広げる 名伸ばす[伸びる]こと, 広がり

□ **string** 名ひも, 糸, 弦

□ **strong** 形①強い, 堅固な, 強烈な ②濃い ③得意な 副強く, 猛烈に

□ **strongly** 副強く, 頑丈に, 猛烈に, 熱心に

□ **struggle** 動 もがく, 奮闘する 名 もがき, 奮闘

□ **student** 名 学生, 生徒

□ **style** 名 やり方, 流儀, 様式, スタイル

□ **submarine** 名 潜水艦 形 海底の

□ **subtropical** 形 亜熱帯の, 亜熱帯性の

□ **such** 形 ①そのような, このような ②そんなに, とても, 非常に 代 そのような人[物] **such as** たとえば～, ～のような

□ **sugar** 名 ①砂糖 ②甘言, お世辞 動 砂糖を入れる, 甘くする

□ **suggest** 動 ①提案する ②示唆する

□ **summer** 名 夏

□ **sunlight** 名 日光

□ **sunshine** 名 日光

□ **supervise** 動 監督する

□ **support** 動 ①支える, 支持する ②養う, 援助する 名 ①支え, 支持 ②援助, 扶養

□ **surrender** 名 降伏, 降参, 明け渡し 動 降伏する, 引き渡す

□ **survive** 動 ①生き残る, 存続する, なんとかなる ②長生きする, 切り抜ける

□ **sway** 動 揺れる, 揺れ動く, 揺すぶる 名 揺れ, 動揺

□ **sweet** 形 甘い

□ **sweetness** 名 ①甘さ ②優しさ, 美しさ

□ **sword** 名 ①剣, 刀 ②武力

□ **symbol** 名 シンボル, 象徴

T

□ **table** 名 ①テーブル, 食卓, 台 ②一覧表 動 卓上に置く, 棚上げにする

□ **tablet** 名 ①タブレット ②銘板

□ **Taiwan** 名 台湾

□ **take** 動 ①取る, 持つ ②持って[連れて]いく, 捕らえる ③乗る ④(時間・労力を)費やす, 必要とする ⑤(ある動作を)する ⑥飲む ⑦耐える, 受け入れる **take care** 気をつける, 注意する **take on** 雇う, (仕事などを)引き受ける **take over** 引き継ぐ, 支配する, 乗っ取る **take place** 行われる, 起こる **take someone in** 身柄を引き取る **take the place of** ～の代わりをする 名 ①取得 ②捕獲

□ **taken** 動 take (取る)の過去分詞

□ **Taketomi Island** 竹富島《石垣島の南に位置する八重山列島の島の一つ》

□ **talent** 名 才能, 才能ある人

□ **talk** 動 話す, 語る, 相談する 名 話, おしゃべり

□ **Tamaudun** 玉陵(たまうどぅん)《那覇市にある琉球王国・第二尚氏王統の歴代国王が葬られている陵墓》

□ **tandiga tandi** たんでぃがーたんでぃ《宮古島の方言で「ありがとう」》

□ **tapas-style** 形 タパス《スペインの小皿料理》スタイルの

□ **tax** 名 ①税 ②重荷, 重い負担 動 ①課税する ②重荷を負わせる

□ **tea** 名 ①茶, 紅茶 ②お茶の会, 午後のお茶

□ **teacher** 名 先生, 教師

□ **teacup** 名 ティーカップ

□ **team** 名 (競技の)組, チーム

□ **tebichi** 名 テビチ《沖縄の方言で「豚足(を煮込んだ料理)」のこと》

□ **technology** 名 テクノロジー, 科学技術

□ **tell** 動 ①話す, 言う, 語る ②教える, 知らせる, 伝える ③わかる, 見分ける

□ **temperature** 名 温度, 体温

□ **temple** 名 寺, 神殿

- **ten** 名 10 (の数字), 10 人 [個] 形 10 の, 10 人 [個] の

- **ten-minute** 10分間の

- **term** 名 ①期間, 期限 ②語, 用語 ③《-s》条件 ④《-s》関係, 仲

- **terrace** 名 台地, テラス, バルコニー

- **textile** 名 布地, 織物, 繊維製品

- **texture** 名 ①手触り, きめ ②織り方, 生地

- **Thai** 形 タイ (人, 語) の 名 ①タイ人 ②タイ語

- **than** 接 〜よりも, 〜以上に **more than** 〜以上 **no more than** ただの 〜にすぎない

- **thank** 動 感謝する, 礼を言う 名 《-s》感謝, 謝意

- **thanks to** 〜のおかげで, 〜の結果

- **that** 形 その, あの **at that time** その時 代 ①それ, あれ, その [あの] 人 [物] ②《関係代名詞》〜である…〜ということ, 〜なので 〜だから **so that** 〜するために, それで, 〜できるように 副 そんなに, それほど

- **the** 冠 ①その, あの ②《形容詞の前で》〜な人々 副 《 − is [are] 〜》〜がある [いる] 名 そこ

- **their** 代 彼 (女) らの, それらの

- **them** 代 彼 (女) らを [に], それらを [に]

- **themselves** 代 彼 (女) ら自身, それら自身

- **then** 副 その時 (に・は), それから, 次に 名 その時 **by then** その時までに 形 その当時の

- **there** 副 ①そこに [で・の], そこへ, あそこへ 《 − is [are] 〜》〜がある [いる] 名 そこ

- **these** 代 これら, これ 形 これらの, この **these days** このごろ

- **they** 代 ①彼 (女) らは [が], それらは [が] ②(一般の) 人々は [が]

- **thick** 形 厚い, 密集した, 濃厚な

- **thickness** 名 厚さ, 太さ, 濃さ

- **thin** 形 薄い, 細い, やせた, まばらな

- **thing** 名 ①物, 事 ②《-s》事情, 事柄 ③《one's -s》持ち物, 身の回り品

- **third-largest** 形 〔規模が〕3番目に大きい, 第3位の

- **this** 形 ①この, こちらの, これを ②今の, 現在の **in this way** このようにして 代 ①これ, この人 [物] ②今, ここ

- **those** 形 それらの, あれらの 代 それら [あれら] の人 [物] **those who** 〜する人々

- **though** 接 ①〜にもかかわらず, 〜だが ②たとえ〜でも **even though** 〜であるけれども, 〜にもかかわらず 副 しかし

- **thought** 動 think (思う) の過去, 過去分詞 名 考え, 意見

- **thread** 名 糸, 糸のように細いもの 動 糸を通す

- **three** 名 3 (の数字), 3 人 [個] 形 3 の, 3 人 [個] の

- **Three-Kingdoms** 名 三山 (時代)《沖縄本島で北山・中山・南山の三王国が割拠していた時代。1322頃 −1429》

- **thrive** 動 よく育つ, 繁栄する

- **through** 前 〜を通して, 〜中を [に], 〜中 副 ①通して ②終りまで, まったく, すっかり **pass through** 〜を通る, 通行する

- **throughout** 前 ①〜中, 〜を通じて ②〜のいたるところに 副 初めから終わりまで, ずっと

- **tile** 名 タイル, 瓦

- **time** 名 ①時, 時間, 歳月 ②時期 ③期間 ④時代 ⑤回, 倍 **at that time** その時 **at times** 時には **each time** 〜するたびに **over time** 時間とともに, そのうち

- **timing** 名 タイミング

119

□ **tip** 图先端, 頂点

□ **to** 前①《方向・変化》~へ, ~に, ~の方へ ②《程度・時間》~まで ③《適合・付加・所属》~に ④《 – + 動詞の原形》~するために[の], ~する, ~すること

□ **today** 图今日 副今日(で)は

□ **tofu** 图豆腐

□ **together** 副①一緒に, ともに ②同時に

□ **Tokyo** 图東京《地名》

□ **toll-free** 形料金のかからない

□ **tomb** 图墓穴, 墓石, 納骨堂

□ **took** 動 take (取る) の過去

□ **top** 形いちばん上の

□ **toss** 動投げる, 放り上げる, 上下に動く

□ **total** 形総計の, 全体の, 完全な 图全体, 合計 動合計する

□ **tour** 图ツアー, 見て回ること, 視察 動(観光)旅行する, 巡業する

□ **tourism** 图①観光旅行, 観光業 ②《集合的》観光客

□ **tourist** 图旅行者, 観光客

□ **towards** 前①《運動の方向・位置》~の方へ, ~に向かって ②《目的》~のために

□ **tower** 图塔

□ **trade** 图取引, 貿易, 商業 動取引する, 貿易する, 商売する

□ **trading** 動 trade (取引する) の現在分詞 图取引, 貿易, 貿易

□ **traditional** 形伝統的な

□ **traffic** 图通行, 往来, 交通(量), 貿易 動商売する, 取引する

□ **training** 動 train (訓練する) の現在分詞 图①トレーニング, 訓練 ②コンディション, 体調

□ **travel** 動①旅行する ②進む, 移動する[させる], 伝わる 图旅行, 運行

□ **traveler** 图旅行者

□ **treasure** 图財宝, 貴重品, 宝物 動秘蔵する

□ **treat** 動①扱う ②治療する ③おごる 图①おごり, もてなし, ごちそう ②楽しみ

□ **treaty** 图条約, 協定 **US-Japan Security Treaty**《the – 》日米安全保障条約

□ **Treaty of San Francisco**《the – 》サンフランシスコ平和条約 图赤, 赤色

□ **tree** 图①木, 樹木, 木製のもの ②系図

□ **trend** 图トレンド, 傾向

□ **tribe** 图部族, 一族

□ **tried** 動 try (試みる) の過去, 過去分詞 形試験済みの, 信頼できる

□ **troop** 图群れ, 隊 動ぞろぞろ歩く, 群れ[列]をなして進む

□ **tropical** 形熱帯の

□ **trouble** 图①困難, 迷惑 ②心配, 苦労 ③もめごと 動①悩ます, 心配させる ②迷惑をかける

□ **trove** 图発見(物), 収集品 **trobe of** ~の宝庫

□ **true** 形①本当の, 本物の, 真の ②誠実な, 確かな 副本当に, 心から

□ **trying** 動 try (やってみる) の現在分詞 形つらい, 苦しい, しゃくにさわる

□ **Tsuboya** 图壷屋《那覇市の地名》

□ **tsumugi** 图紬《紬糸で織られた絹織物》

□ **Tsurumi** 图鶴見《神奈川県の地区名》

□ **Tsushima Maru** 対馬丸《日本郵船の貨物船。1944年8月22日, 学童疎開の輸送中にアメリカ海軍の攻撃を受けて沈没》

□ **tube** 图管, 筒

□ **turn** 動①ひっくり返す, 回転する[させる], 曲がる, 曲げる, 向かう, 向ける ②(~に)なる, (~に)変える

turn into ～に変わる

□ **turning** 動 turn（ひっくり返す）の現在分詞 名 回転, 曲がり角

□ **twentieth** 名《the ～》第20（の人・物）形《the ～》第20の, 20番の

□ **two** 名 2（の数字）, 2人［個］形 2の, 2人［個］の

□ **type** 名 ①型, タイプ, 様式 ②見本, 模様, 典型 動 ①典型となる ②タイプで打つ

□ **typical** 形 典型的な, 象徴的な

□ **typhoon** 名 台風

U

□ **Uchinanchu** 名 うちなーんちゅ《沖縄の方言で「沖縄の人」という意味》

□ **Uken shell mounds** 宇堅貝塚《沖縄県うるま市字宇堅にある貝塚群》

□ **umi budo** 海ぶどう《沖縄の海に生息する「クビレズタ」のこと》

□ **unable** 形《be - to ～》～することができない

□ **under** 前 ①《位置》～の下［に］②《状態》～で, ～を受けて, ～のもと ③《数量》～以下［未満］の, ～より下の 形 下の, 下部の 副 下に［で］, 従属［服従］して

□ **underwater** 形 水面下の, 水中（用）の 副 水面下で, 水中で

□ **UNESCO** 名（＝ United Nations Educational, Scientific and Cultural Organization）国際連合教育科学文化機関, ユネスコ

□ **UNESCO Intangible Cultural Heritage** ユネスコ無形文化遺産

□ **UNESCO World Heritage Site** ユネスコ世界遺産

□ **unfair** 形 不公平な, 不当な

□ **unfortunately** 副 不幸にも, 運悪く

□ **unique** 形 唯一の, ユニークな, 独自の

□ **unite** 動 ①1つにする［なる］, 合わせる, 結ぶ ②結束する, 団結する

□ **United States Civil Administration of the Ryukyu Islands** 琉球列島米国民政府《略称として USCAR（ユースカー）と呼ばれる》

□ **unknown** 形 知られていない, 不明の

□ **unlike** 形 似ていない, 違った 前 ～と違って

□ **until** 前 ～まで（ずっと）接 ～の時まで, ～するまで

□ **untouched** 形 そのままの, 触られていない

□ **up** 副 ①上へ, 上がって, 北へ ②立って, 近づいて ③向上して, 増して **be made up of** ～で構成されている **break up** ばらばらになる, 解散させる **make up** 作り出す, 考え出す, ～を構成［形成］する **pile up** 積み重ねる **set up** 設置する, 定める **up to** ～まで, ～に至るまで, ～に匹敵して 前 ①～の上（の方）へ, 高い方へ ②（道）に沿って 形 上向きの, 上りの

□ **upon** 前 ①《場所・接触》～（の上）に ②《日・時》～に ③《関係・従事》～に関して, ～について, ～して

□ **Urauchi River** 浦内川《西表島中央部を流れる沖縄県内で最長の河川》

□ **urge** 動 ①せき立てる, 強力に推し進める, かりたてる ②《… to ～》…に～するよう熱心に勧める 名 衝動, かりたてられるような気持ち

□ **Uruma city** うるま市《沖縄本島中部に位置する県内第3の都市》

□ **US** アメリカ合衆国（＝ United States）

□ **US-Japan Security Treaty** 《the ～》日米安全保障条約

□ **use** 動 ①使う, 用いる ②費やす 名 使用, 用途

□ **used** 動 ①use (使う) の過去, 過去分詞 ②《- to》よく～したものだ, 以前は～であった 形 ①慣れている, 《get [become] - to》～に慣れてくる ②使われた, 中古の

□ **usually** 副 普通に, いつも (は)

□ **utaki** 名 御嶽《琉球信仰における聖域。神話の神や祖先神を祀る祭祀の場》

V

□ **valuable** 形 貴重な, 価値のある, 役に立つ

□ **value** 名 価値, 値打ち, 価格 動 評価する, 値をつける, 大切にする

□ **various** 形 変化に富んだ, さまざまの, たくさんの

□ **vary** 動 変わる, 変える, 変更する, 異なる

□ **vast** 形 広大な, 巨大な, ばく大な

□ **vegetable** 名 野菜, 青物 形 野菜の, 植物 (性) の

□ **version** 名 ①バージョン, 版, 翻訳 ②意見, 説明, 解釈

□ **very** 副 とても, 非常に, まったく 形 本当の, きわめて, まさしくその

□ **victory** 名 勝利, 優勝

□ **Vietnam** 名 ベトナム《国名》

□ **view** 名 ①眺め, 景色, 見晴らし ②考え方, 意見 動 眺める

□ **village** 名 村, 村落

□ **visit** 動 訪問する 名 訪問

□ **visitor** 名 訪問客

□ **volume** 名 ①《-s》たくさん, 多量 ②量, 容積

□ **voyage** 動 航海する, 空の旅をする

W

□ **walk** 動 歩く, 歩かせる, 散歩する **walk along** ～に沿って歩く **walk around** 歩き回る, ぶらぶら歩く 名 歩くこと, 散歩

□ **walking** 動 walk (歩く) の現在分詞 名 歩行, 歩くこと

□ **wall** 名 ①壁, 塀 ②障壁 動 壁 [塀] で囲む, ふさぐ

□ **wallet** 名 札入れ

□ **want** 動 ほしい, 望む, ～したい, ～してほしい 名 欠乏, 不足

□ **wanting** 動 want (ほしい) の現在分詞 形 欠けている

□ **war** 名 戦争 (状態), 闘争, 不和

□ **warm** 形 ①暖かい, 温暖な ②思いやりのある, 愛情のある 動 暖まる, 暖める **warm current** 暖流

□ **was** 動 《be の第1・第3人称単数現在 am, is の過去》～であった, (～に) いた [あった]

□ **wash** 動 ①洗う, 洗濯する ②押し流す [される] **wash away** 押し流す 名 洗うこと

□ **washtub** 名 洗濯用たらい

□ **watch** 動 ①じっと見る, 見物する ②注意 [用心] する, 監視する **watch over** 見守る, 見張る 名 ①警戒, 見張り ②腕時計

□ **water** 名 ①水 ②《川・湖・海などの》多量の水 動 水を飲ませる, (植物に) 水をやる

□ **wave** 名 波

□ **way** 名 ①道, 通り道 ②方向, 距離 ③方法, 手段 ④習慣 **in this way** このようにして **way of** ～する方法 **way of life** 生き様, 生き方, 暮らし方

□ **we** 代 私たちは [が]

□ **weak** 形 ①弱い, 力のない, 病弱な ②劣った, へたな, 苦手な

□ **wear** 動①着る, 着ている, 身につける ②疲れる, 消耗する, すり切れる 名①着用 ②衣類

□ **weather** 名天気, 天候, 空模様

□ **weaving** 動 weave (織機で布を織る) の現在分詞

□ **welcome** 動歓迎する

□ **well** 副①うまく, 上手に ②十分に, よく, かなり **as well as** ～と同様に 形健康な, 適当な, 申し分ない

□ **well-known** 形よく知られた, 有名な

□ **well-off** 形①裕福な, 富裕な ②順調な, 恵まれた

□ **were** 動《beの2人称単数・複数の過去》～であった, (～に) いた [あった]

□ **west** 名《the –》西, 西部, 西方, 《the W-》西洋 形西の, 西方 [西部] の, 西向きの 副西に, 西方へ

□ **western** 形西の, 西側の

□ **Western Pacific** 西太平洋

□ **whale-watching** クジラの観察, ホエール・ウォッチング

□ **what** 代①何が [を・に] ②《関係代名詞》～するところのもの [こと] 形①何の, どんな ②なんて ③～するだけの 副いかに, どれほど

□ **wheat** 名小麦

□ **when** 副①いつ ②《関係副詞》～するところの, ～するとその時, ～するとき 接～の時, ～するとき 代いつ

□ **where** 副①どこに [で] ②《関係副詞》～するところの, そしてそこで, ～するところ 接～なところに [へ], ～するところに [へ] 代①どこ, どの点 ②～するところの

□ **whether** 接～かどうか, ～かまたは…, ～であろうとなかろうと

□ **which** 形①どちらの, どの, どれでも ②どんな～でも, そしてこの 代①どちら, どれ, どの人 [物] ②《関係代名詞》～するところの **of which**

～の中で

□ **while** 接①～の間 (に), ～する間 (に) ②一方, ～なのに 名しばらくの間, 一定の時

□ **white** 形①白い, (顔色などが) 青ざめた ②白人の 名白, 白色

□ **who** 代①誰が [は], どの人 ②《関係代名詞》～するところの (人) **those who** ～する人々

□ **whole** 形全体の, すべての, 完全な, 満～, 丸～ 名《the –》全体, 全部 **as a whole** 全体として

□ **why** 副①なぜ, どうして ②《関係副詞》～するところの (理由) 間①おや, まあ ②もちろん, なんだって ③ええっ

□ **wide** 形幅の広い, 広範囲の, 幅が～ある 副広く, 大きく開いて

□ **wild** 形①野生の ②荒涼として ③荒っぽい ④奇抜な

□ **will** 助～だろう, ～しよう, する (つもりだ) 名決意, 意図

□ **wind** 名①風 ②うねり, 一巻き 動巻く, からみつく, うねる

□ **winning** 動 win (勝つ) の現在分詞 名勝つこと, 勝利, 《-s》賞金 形勝った, 優勝の

□ **winter** 名冬 動冬を過ごす

□ **wisdom** 名知恵, 賢明 (さ)

□ **wish** 動望む, 願う, (～であればよいと) 思う 名 (心からの) 願い

□ **with** 前①《同伴・付随・所属》～と一緒に, ～を身につけて, ～とともに ②《様態》～ (の状態) で, ～して ③《手段・道具》～で, ～を使って **along with** ～と一緒に

□ **without** 前～なしで, ～がなく, ～しないで

□ **women** 名 woman (女性) の複数

□ **won't** will not の短縮形

□ **woodpecker** 名《鳥》キツツキ

□ **word** 名語, 単語

□ **work** 動①働く, 勉強する, 取り組

む ②機能［作用］する，うまくいく
work hard 一生懸命に［せっせと］
働く **work in** 〜の分野で働く，〜に
入り込む **work out** 考え出す，答え
が出る，〜の結果になる 图①仕事，
勉強 ②職 ③作品

□ **working** 動work（働く）の現在分
詞 形働く，作業の，実用的な

□ **world** 图《the –》世界，〜界
world of 大量の，無数の

□ **World War II** 第二次世界大戦

□ **Worldwide Uchinanchu
Festival** 世界のウチナーンチュ大
会《沖縄出身の海外移民とその家族を
招待する国際交流イベント》

□ **worse** 形いっそう悪い，より劣っ
た，よりひどい 副いっそう悪く

□ **worship** 图崇拝，礼拝，参拝 動崇
拝する，礼拝［参拝］する，拝む

□ **would** 助《willの過去》①〜する
だろう，〜するつもりだ ②〜したも
のだ

□ **write down** 書き留める

□ **writing** 動write（書く）の現在分
詞 图①書くこと，作文，著述 ②書き
物，書かれたもの，文書

□ **written** 動write（書く）の過去分
詞 形文書の，書かれた

□ **wrong** 形①間違った，(道徳上）悪
い ②調子が悪い，故障した 副間違
って 图不正，悪事

Y

□ **yachimun** 图やちむん《沖縄の方
言で「沖縄の焼き物・陶器」のこと》

□ **Yaeyama Islands** 八重山列島
《南西諸島西部の島嶼群》

□ **Yanbaru forest** やんばるの森《沖
縄本島の北部地域に広がる森林》

□ **year** 图①年，1年 ②学年，年度 ③
〜歳 **all year** 一年中，一年を通して
for 〜 years 〜年間，〜年にわたって

New Year's Day 元日

□ **year-round** 形年間を通した 副
一年中，年間を通して，通年で

□ **yen** 图円《日本の通貨単位》

□ **yet** 副①《否定文で》まだ〜（ない［し
ない]）②《疑問文で》もう ③《肯定
文で》まだ，今もなお 接それにもか
かわらず，しかし，けれども

□ **Yomitan** 图読谷（村）《沖縄本島中
部に位置する村》

□ **Yomitanza** 图読谷山《読谷村の旧
地域名》

□ **Yonaguni Island** 与那国島《八
重山列島に属する日本最西端の島》

□ **you** 代①あなた（方）は［が]，あな
た（方）を［に]②（一般に）人は

□ **young** 形若い，幼い，青年の

□ **Yukka Nu Hii** ユッカヌヒー《沖
縄の方言で「旧暦5月4日」を指す》

□ **yushi dofu** ゆし豆腐《にがりを加
えて固まりはじめのふわふわした豆
腐のこと》

Z

□ **Zakimi Castle** 座喜味城《読谷村
にある城跡。築城の名人といわれた読
谷山按司・護佐丸によって築かれた》

English Conversational Ability Test
国際英語会話能力検定

● E-CATとは…
英語が話せるようになるための
テストです。インターネット
ベースで、30分であなたの発
話力をチェックします。

www.ecatexam.com

● iTEP®とは…
世界各国の企業、政府機関、アメリカの大学
300校以上が、英語能力判定テストとして採用。
オンラインによる90分のテストで文法、リー
ディング、リスニング、ライティング、スピー
キングの5技能をスコア化。iTEP®は、留学、就
職、海外赴任などに必要な、世界に通用する英
語力を総合的に評価する画期的なテストです。

www.itepexamjapan.com

［著者紹介］

小林 悠樹（こばやし ゆうき）

フリーライター。1988年神奈川県生まれ、一橋大学商学部卒業。冷凍食品メーカー、編集プロダクションでの勤務を経て、2017年フリーランスとして独立。現在は沖縄県宮古島市を拠点に、ウェブサイト・書籍の原稿執筆をおこなう。

［訳者紹介］

Kamil Spychalski（カミール スパイチャルスキ）

ポーランド出身、7歳でオーストラリアに渡る。西オーストラリア大学を卒業後福岡に移住し、福岡県国際交流センター（2011〜2016）における勤務を経てフリーランス翻訳者となる。大手日本企業の広報の翻訳に従事するほか、出版・文芸翻訳も視野に入れる。第10回JAT（日本翻訳者協会）新人翻訳者コンテスト日英翻訳部門第一位。

ラダーシリーズ

Exploring Okinawa　英語で読む沖縄

2020年3月4日　第1刷発行

著　者　　小林　悠樹

発行者　　浦　　晋亮

発行所　　**IBCパブリッシング株式会社**
　　　　　〒162-0804 東京都新宿区中里町29番3号
　　　　　菱秀神楽坂ビル9F
　　　　　Tel. 03-3513-4511　Fax. 03-3513-4512
　　　　　www.ibcpub.co.jp

印刷　中央精版印刷株式会社

装丁　伊藤 理恵

落丁本・乱丁本は、小社宛にお送りください。送料小社負担にてお取り替えいたします。本書の無断複写（コピー）は著作権法上での例外を除き禁じられています。

Printed in Japan
ISBN978-4-7946-0620-4